MEMORY
BUILDERS

Other Books by Frank Minirth

Happiness Is a Choice
Introduction to Psychology and Counseling
A Brilliant Mind
Choosing Happiness When Life Is Hard
Boost Your Brainpower
You Can!

MEMORY BUILDERS

*Easy Exercises
to Sharpen
Your Memory*

FRANK MINIRTH, MD

SPIRE

© 2017 by Minirth Holdings, LLC

Published by Revell
a division of Baker Publishing Group
PO Box 6287, Grand Rapids, MI 49516-6287
www.revellbooks.com

Spire edition published 2021
ISBN 978-0-8007-3958-4

Previously published in 2017 as *Strong Memory, Sharp Mind*

Printed in the United States of America

The names and details of the people and situations described in this book have been changed or presented in composite form in order to ensure the privacy of those with whom the author has worked.

This publication is intended to provide helpful and informative material on the subjects addressed. Readers should consult their personal health professionals before adopting any of the suggestions in this book or drawing inferences from it. The author and publisher expressly disclaim responsibility for any adverse effects arising from the use or application of the information contained in this book.

21   22   23   24   25   26   27   7   6   5   4   3   2   1

I dedicate this book
to all who seek to guard their minds
and to caretakers of those in mental decline—
as a personal encouragement,
as a source for information and help,
and as a timely call to action.

Dr. Frank Minirth was a pioneer in Christian psychiatry. He posthumously received the inaugural Frank B. Minirth Christian Psychiatry and Behavioral Medicine Award by the American Association of Christian Counselors in 2015.

Contents

Contents

How to Use This Book

Brain on Board

You don't see it or feel it. You can't hear it or hold it.
It's out of sight, out of mind.
Don't drift through your thirties, forties, and fifties,
then suddenly realize your brain is fading.
Don't settle for it being just "good enough."
You deserve better than that.
Don't take your brain for granted.

I wrote this book for those who want a basic understanding of the brain's strengths and vulnerabilities and what can be done to reduce the risk of mental decline. My hope is that the content will motivate you to take personal action to keep your mind sharp.

I've included many lists throughout this book because it's the best way to package a lot of information so it can be processed and retained by the brain. Scan the lists and stop on the items that catch your attention. Some repetition exists because repetition helps learning.

I've designed this book as a personal workbook for readers of all ages and as a caregiver's handbook. It's a helpful resource for every person, family, counselor, care center, health-care provider, senior citizen group, and mental health-care agency.

Keep a Pen and Highlighter Handy

I encourage you to mark meaningful passages for frequent review and to highlight the action tips and how-to lists. Noting these will provide a good basis for making a personalized "brain-care action plan." Keep refreshing the plan by reviewing this book for more ideas.

It's also important to engage in the Brain Boosters mental exercises. They are designed to be reviewed over and over because cognition works through repetition. Learning broad knowledge rekindles and increases memory tracks. If you have difficulty with some of the exercises, don't quit. Researching the answers will help you retain the knowledge. Keep studying and repeating these exercises until you master them with speed and accuracy. The answers can be found in appendix D.

Brain Fitness Is a Ticket to a More Vital Life

I encourage everyone, whether you're thirty or sixty or eighty, to take this book to heart because a mind is a terrible thing to lose. Every individual has to make the personal choice to protect his or her memory for a better chance to make it through old age with an intact, robust mind. In this case, choices really do matter. Don't let each birthday mark more lost memories, diminished skills, and waning relationships. Life's many opportunities and blessings can drift away with age if the brain isn't nourished and exercised.

Note

Medical information about the brain changes at a rapid rate. What is thought to be true today may be better elucidated tomorrow, so errors are possible. Never disregard or delay seeking medical advice because of something heard from the media, read in a book, or seen on the internet.

Some of the content of this book is technical, but readers will glean a greater awareness of and appreciation for the complexity, vulnerabilities, and miraculous powers of the human brain.

This book is not intended as a specific guide for any medical diagnosis or treatment; medical doctors should be consulted for all medical conditions. It includes general references to common information. When deciding on specifics of any medical actions, symptoms, diagnoses, prognoses, or treatments, many aspects must be considered. The information given here may not be absolute or complete; variations, coinciding factors, and updates may exist.

Introduction

Memory Matters

At birthday celebrations, I hear phrases such as "the thirties are the new twenties," "the forties are the new thirties," and "the fifties are the new forties." People brag about looking and feeling younger than their parents did at the same chronological age.

We want our minds to stay dynamic too. But after high school or college, some people never pick up another book or take another class. The more fit we keep our brains, the better they'll withstand the rigors of aging, protect our well-being, and lead to life satisfaction.

Everyone wants to be happy, healthy, loved, and reasonably prosperous and to enjoy fulfilling relationships. These core desires keep us motivated. Our decisions are based on these desires as well as habits, others' demands, impulsive urges, and conscious planning. And every day we choose what thoughts to dwell on and words to say, and what to do and not do. Each choice has far-reaching ramifications. Bit by bit, we form patterns that direct our lives and interpersonal interactions.

Something you may have not considered is that none of this is possible without a healthy brain. Your mind controls behavior, and if your mental status is compromised, days, weeks, months, and years can be difficult for you and your family.

I hope this book will motivate you to refresh healthy choices and to follow through with a brain-care action plan. Keep modifying the plan along the way as you age and life events change. It's okay to start with the easiest steps. Just start.

Don't Just Let Nature Take Its Course

If you've hit your early thirties, your brain's natural aging process has started. It may take longer to memorize and learn new things, and your verbal fluency, perception, and reasoning skills are slowing down.

Changes in the mind and body continue through every life phase. But the older we get, the more dramatic the symptoms seem: our hair and skin look different, and memories often begin to fade. This impacts everyone at some point, but there is help and hope to keep our minds intact through the senior years.

What are your concerns and goals? The sooner you start taking the memory-care steps suggested in this book, the more progress and positive outcomes you'll experience as the years pass. You can stay sharp mentally by exercising and nurturing the wondrous infrastructure of your brain.

There is a broad spectrum of brain function. During the typical life span, brain function starts high and decreases as risk factors take their toll:

(1) From a superior functioning brain → (2) to average cognition → (3) to a slight decrease in cognition → (4) to early cognitive decline → (5) to minor neurocognitive dysfunction → (6) to major neurocognitive dysfunction.

Where do you think you are in this process now? Where would you like to be? This book can help you get there. Don't regret that you didn't act sooner. Early detection of mental decline is the key to a better long-term prognosis.

Do You Want a Sharper Mind? It's Possible at Any Age

When one of my daughters was young, I asked, "Do you want to boost your brainpower?" She did. Today, she is a medical doctor and psychiatrist.

In response to a frail, elderly pastor's request for help with his fading memory, I asked, "Do you want to boost your brainpower?" He did. He has returned to preaching and is enjoying a thriving ministry.

It's encouraging to know that brainpower can be increased at any age—through childhood, adolescence, young adulthood, adulthood, and even in the senior years. The benefits of controlling, challenging, directing, and improving our minds are many, including delaying cognitive decline or slowing the progression of Alzheimer's disease.

The choices you make over your lifetime can be fateful or fruitful. Making the necessary choices to preserve your long-term brainpower is solely up to you. Nobody can do it for you. This book empowers you with scientific facts, timely information, and many how-to tips in self-help action plans. Believe you can improve your memory. Most everyone can if they put in the effort and believe they can. In a renowned psychology study, teachers told a group of average students that they were gifted in intellect and memory (they were not). By the end of the school year they were at the top of their classes due to embracing learning and growth opportunities. Believing in their potential and capabilities made a difference. Learning shouldn't stop after the three thousand days of school before high school graduation.

In fact, the next twenty to forty years spent building your career, raising a family, and setting yourself up for eventual retirement are the most critical years for developing and preserving your brain. Because you're reading this book you're obviously already aware of the profound benefits of brain fitness, and you're off to a great start.

This Book Is Your Brain-Care Owner's Manual

The care and feeding of your brain are critical. Rest it. Feed it. Exercise it. Teach it. Challenge it. Protect it. Fight for it. Build it. Stimulate it. Fuel it. Water it. Cross-train it. Entertain it. Flex it. Work it. Preserve it.

Each chapter of this book concludes with a Choose Well section that will help you enjoy more confidence and success throughout your adult years. The Brain Boosters mental exercises provide a sampling of the kinds of knowledge that can strengthen your memory. I've drawn from professional and scientific research and from personal training and experience to write this book. Please use it as a workbook. Write in it and turn down corners of key pages for frequent review. I believe that your efforts will not only benefit you now but will also help preserve your high-functioning brain through the years ahead. This is my hope for you.

A Personal Note

When I graduated from medical school, I took the Hippocratic Oath, which is traditional for physicians as they begin medical practice. Several phrases from that pledge have inspired me throughout my career to promote preventive mental health care to help people avoid or lessen the devastating effects of mental illness.

Here are some excerpts:

I will prevent disease whenever I can for prevention is preferable to cure.

I will remember that I remain a member of society, with special obligations to all my fellow human beings, those sound of mind and body as well as the infirm.

The books I've written and the years of hosting radio talk shows were in response to these commitments. I have focused on educating people about mental health so they can be aware of and recognize problems in the early stages. This book is my continued "call to action" to encourage everyone to protect their mind and their long-term quality of life.

Dr. Frank Minirth

PART 1

Threats to Cognitive Health

1

It's Your Choice

IT'S A FACT: The brain directs all thinking, feeling, moving, talking, and activity. It's never too early or too late to take care of your brain . . . so it can take care of you.

Memory is the guardian of all things.
Cicero, circa 70 BC

We are what we repeatedly do.
Aristotle, 350 BC

Without memory you wouldn't know how to drive to work. Without memory you wouldn't recognize your family. Without memory you couldn't even talk. Without your memory there would be no you. Without memory there's no brainpower.

There is profound truth in Aristotle's timeless adage. I would alter that statement just a little to say, "We often become what we want to become by what we repeatedly choose to do." What we repeatedly put into our brains helps determine who we are, how we think, and what we do. Aristotle's adage serves as a wake-up call to consider our good as well as our bad routines and habits. Are these choices helping or hurting us?

Everyone knows that our bodies perform better when they're regularly nourished and exercised. Muscle cells develop with repeated physical exercise. We lift weights to build muscle and do sit-ups to strengthen abs. The same is true for our brains; they need regular workouts too.

Brain cell connections are developed and maintained with repeated mental exercise. Exercise increases brain cell dendrite connections to other brain cells and revitalizes brain circuits. The phrase "use it or lose it" applies to the neural pathways and connections in our brains as much as it does to our muscles. Each mental challenge builds new associations among the neural connections of the brain.

Your choices chart your life, for better or worse. If you're in your thirties or forties, you've got the time, momentum, and some life experience going for you. To be healthy, your brain needs regular exercise, rest, nutrition, and tune-ups. Daily choices can be just as important as the major decisions you make. Are your lifestyle choices hurting or helping your brain health?

Take this quick quiz.

	Yes	No
Do you eat junk food and sugar?	___	___
Do you sit the majority of the day?	___	___
Do you spend hours watching television or surfing the internet?	___	___

	Yes	No
Do you generally feel stressed or anxious?	___	___
Do you spend more time watching television than reading books or exercising?	___	___
Do you spend most of your days alone?	___	___
Do you have a chronic illness?	___	___
Do you have an unhealthy addiction?	___	___
Do you have a weight problem?	___	___
Do you get less than seven hours of sleep at night?	___	___

The more yes answers you have, the more you may need a brain-care tune-up.

Why Do You Want a Sharper Mind?

Place a check mark by all the following motives that apply to you. This will encourage you to step up your brain fitness. It may also help you clarify your short- and long-range goals, strengths, and areas for improvement.

I want to build my brainpower so I can

___ decrease the chance of memory loss in later years

___ maintain my current level of memory and brain function

___ improve my self-esteem

___ maintain independence as long as possible

___ improve my decision-making and problem-solving skills

___ facilitate my career advancement

___ improve my short- and long-term memory

___ avoid embarrassing situations (i.e., brain freeze, senior moments)

___ improve my attention span and concentration

_____ improve my scholastic performance

_____ do more multitasking (which is really changing sharp focus very quickly)

_____ be more efficient in daily routines

_____ consistently function at my best level

_____ improve my relationships

_____ function better in business and social situations (i.e., remember names and details)

_____ reduce the stress of managing all my responsibilities

_____ accentuate my personal strengths

_____ have more intelligent conversations

_____ enjoy more special interests and activities

_____ stop or reverse cognitive decline (cognition is the mental process of acquiring knowledge and understanding through thought, experience, and the senses)

Consider the consequences if you choose to do nothing to boost your brain. All of the incentives listed above may be at risk. It may seem tough to take on a brain-care action plan, but it's going to be even tougher in the long run to ignore it. The sobering realization is that your brain is vulnerable to a natural decrease in function.

You can do something about this decline with a little effort and commitment. Brain care can be done in small steps over a period of time. It's unique in the fact that it's doable for people of all ages and varying circumstances.

Don't let apathy get in the way of becoming who you want to be now and through your senior years. Excuses and procrastination are your enemies. Rarely is anyone successful without hard work. Apathy is a symptom of certain medical conditions, including depression and dementia. If you lacked motivation and interest, you probably wouldn't be reading this book, so it's not too late for you.

As you continue reading, highlight all the action tips that might interest you for a brain-care plan. Start small. Just start. You'll be glad you did. These choices will improve the quality of your life now and in the future.

Make Willpower Work for You

God created you with a will—an ability to choose. This is key. With your willpower, you can continually move toward balanced, healthy behaviors such as physical and mental exercise, a nutritious diet, and spiritual growth.

But before you can achieve and enjoy this balance, you may have some unhealthy behaviors that need to be limited or stopped. Do you drink too much alcohol, smoke, take drugs, lack sleep, rarely exercise, or overeat? Maybe you need to practice some "won't power" too. These common lifestyle challenges require a personal act of will, a personal choice, to overcome.

Do you argue with yourself when it comes to problems of willpower? It's in our nature.

As a medical doctor for over forty years, I've repeatedly seen people move toward better choices because of willpower. The choice factor is significant in their overall well-being. I've seen people choose to stop addictions, focus better, eat more appropriately, become less depressed, and act more appropriately. They often receive caring help to do so, but the choice is theirs. Sometimes willpower can reign over stress factors and, to a degree, even genetics and disease symptoms.

I'm not saying that stress and other epigenetic factors (external modifications to DNA that turn genes on or off) aren't important. I'm not saying that medical factors in the genome are unimportant. I'm saying that choices can be a significant factor in moving toward self-improvement and better health, as well as a healthier and happier outlook.

Training your brain to receive and act on the suggestion of your willpower takes practice. Part of the challenge will be to overcome bouts of doubt and a constant barrage of distractions. These obstacles will challenge your willpower every day. Without a reasonable plan, a personal commitment, and even a support system or accountability partner, there's little chance for lasting improvement.

I had a former neighbor who lacked self-discipline and willpower in his personal life. He functioned at work but was stymied by bad habits and apathy at home. He was disorganized, left home projects unfinished, and had no desire to try anything new or challenging. His children were grown, and his wife had passed away. His mental and physical health declined, but he refused medical care. Lonely and depressed, he passed away after a brief illness.

You may know someone like this. But even people like him can find new hope through developing their willpower. It's the basis for good health, a balanced lifestyle, and personal success.

It's not easy to gain power over bad habits and unhealthy desires. Did you know that it usually takes about twenty-one days to establish a habit? Beyond that point, it becomes easier and even more entrenched as it is repeated.

It's also not easy to change or manage our core personality traits. The way we think and act is partly influenced by the brain's structures, hormones, neurotransmitters, and patterns of brain activity. Sometimes our natural personality traits are positive assets; sometimes they're stumbling blocks. But what's important is that we aim to develop the positive traits and overcome the negative ones.

Managing our cognitive styles is a brain function challenge. With your willpower, you can lessen the intensity of some of your undesirable personality traits.

Check any negative trait(s) that may apply to you:

___ demanding, controlling, perfectionistic, stubborn, indecisive

___ emotional, excitable, egocentric

___ grandiose preoccupation with self

___ dramatic, conflict-oriented relationships, impulsive, angry

___ suspicious, hypersensitive, mistrusting of people

___ unstable moods and friendships, self-identity problems, nonconforming

___ shy, hypersensitive to rejection, socially withdrawn

___ overly dependent on others

___ procrastinating, inefficient

___ aloof

Scripture Power

In addition to your choices and willpower, there is a mighty power available to help you on your journey. I'll tell you about one of the most powerful forces on earth—power not only in the spiritual world but also in the intellectual world. Power that has protected me. Power that is both pragmatic and abstract. Power I simply call "Scripture Power."

It is much more than intellectual. I've seen this power work in my life in different ways: direct empowerment by God, direction, discipline, discernment, diversion from sin, increased intellectual ability, joy, and correction, to name just a few.

The Bible is the number-one-selling book of all time, the greatest book ever written. The Bible is not of this world, it is "God-breathed." When I reflect on God's Word, I think about its rich history—it's still inerrant, infallible, and inalienable after thousands of years. God was the author through forty human writers; sixty-six books are miraculously one book. This timeless Scripture ranges from the history of human-kind, to relevance for today, to hope for tomorrow.

Although the accounts of people in the Bible were divinely inspired, the individuals were mere mortals with similar strengths, weaknesses, and personal struggles we experience today. We can identify with them and learn lessons from their lives that help us cope with the stresses of the twenty-first century.

The societies in which these biblical characters lived were vastly different from ours—no technology or mass transportation and limited scientific knowledge. They didn't face such things as the threat of nuclear warfare, but their timely concerns were as real to them as ours are to us. They grappled with similar life-and-death issues. Accounts of their lives and how God works in and among us provide lessons that can guide our choices today.

The Bible teaches both individual choice and God's sovereignty. Choice and sovereignty don't negate each other. God wants us to make good choices; this book can guide you through some of them.

Choose Well

There's a lot to be said for motivation, common sense, and mental fitness. They serve you well in everything you do.

As much as possible, choose to stay in a healthy zone—mentally, physically, emotionally, and spiritually. Being in constant pursuit of self-improvement is a process that requires a series of good choices. There is truth in the adage "We make our choices, then our choices make us."

Self-Assessment—How Am I Doing?

When evaluating your personal brain health, the following factors can guide you. This is a snapshot of current stressors that may be impeding your mental and physical health.

Note: This brief self-assessment may be influenced by your current state of mind, depending on whether you are feeling confident or stressed out. Consider each of the following issues from an honest, general, insightful viewpoint.

Place a check mark by each of the areas that you may need help with or may need some improvement in your life:

___	general functioning	___	diet
___	illness	___	job performance
___	relationships	___	energy level
___	addictions	___	productivity
___	medications/drugs	___	weight
___	mood	___	sensitivity
___	healthy choices	___	decision making
___	exercise	___	stress level
___	learning new things	___	time management

_____ memory/cognition	_____ financial security
_____ business arrangements	_____ confusion
_____ anxiety	_____ sleep habits
_____ pain level	_____ appearance/grooming
_____ hobbies	_____ codependency (addiction to people, behaviors, or things)
_____ major, recent events/ changes	_____ personality traits
_____ family history	_____ technology/TV habits
_____ abuse	_____ self-esteem
_____ wasting time	_____ other issues
_____ attitude	
_____ physical symptoms	

Select the Brain Boosters You Will Start This Week

Although they appear to be simple, the following are designed to exercise specific cognitive functions of your brain.

_____ Learn more about something that interests you. (Education increases dendritic fields in the cortical language area.)

_____ Read something mentally stimulating at least thirty minutes daily (novels, books about hobbies and special interests, newspapers for current events). Occasionally read out loud.

_____ Create a more stimulating environment at home.

_____ Take new routes when you drive or go for walks.

_____ Spend more time with friends for stimulating social interactions.

_____ Learn new vocabulary words each week and use them in daily conversation (see appendix C).

_____ Play board games, chess, and cards; do puzzles.

_____ Play video games or explore the internet on topics of interest.

_____ Comb your hair and brush your teeth with the opposite hand.

_____ Listen to music and learn the lyrics to new songs.

_____ Make changes in the order of daily routines.

_____ Take ten- to fifteen-minute power naps. (Brains at rest can help organize information and memories.)

_____ Take a free class at a local library or college.

_____ Focus on five items in a room, then try to recall those items throughout the day, especially when you have changed to a different location.

_____ Do stretching exercises during television commercials.

Now ask yourself: Do I honestly feel that my routines and choices are healthy? Would the people I trust say my actions and choices are healthy?

Brain Boosters

Fact: Increasing mental exercise improves cognition.

The more years you consistently stimulate your memory the better chance you have of reducing the threat of cognitive decline or dementia. If you are thirty years old and start right now, you may be able to accomplish years or decades of preventive care. Investing this effort for a vital mind is similar to the money you're already investing for a comfortable retirement lifestyle. Try the following mental exercises.

Abstract Puzzle

A man is looking at a portrait on a wall and says, "Brothers and sisters I have none, but this man's father is my father's son." At whose portrait is he looking?[1]

Memorization

Memorize the forty-five US presidents in order. List them as quickly as you can and repeat them daily: Washington, Adams, Jefferson, Madison, Monroe, Adams, Jackson, Van Buren, Harrison, Tyler, Polk, Taylor, Fillmore, Pierce, Buchanan, Lincoln, Johnson, Grant, Hayes, Garfield, Arthur, Cleveland, Harrison, Cleveland, McKinley, Roosevelt, Taft, Wilson, Harding, Coolidge, Hoover, Roosevelt, Truman, Eisenhower, Kennedy, Johnson, Nixon, Ford, Carter, Reagan, Bush, Clinton, Bush, Obama, Trump.

When you've mastered that, try learning and practicing them in reverse order: Trump, Obama, Bush, Clinton, Bush, Reagan, Carter, Ford, Nixon, Johnson, Kennedy, Eisenhower, Truman, Roosevelt, Hoover, Coolidge, Harding, Wilson, Taft, Roosevelt, McKinley, Cleveland, Harrison, Cleveland, Arthur, Garfield, Hayes, Grant, Johnson, Lincoln, Buchanan, Pierce, Fillmore, Taylor, Polk, Tyler, Harrison, Van Buren, Jackson, Adams, Monroe, Madison, Jefferson, Adams, Washington.

If you're not interested in learning the presidents, make a list of thirty to forty items in a topic that relates to your profession or hobbies and memorize that list.

Math Exercises

Practice math exercises in your head when you go for a walk or while you wait in the car.

- Calculating tips for staff at restaurants, airports, hotels, beauty shops, and other places is a daily challenge. Impress your friends and ditch your smartphone calculator.

     Find 10 percent of the total bill by moving the decimal to the left one space.

     5 percent is half that amount.

     For 15 percent, add the 10 and 5 percent.

     20 percent is double the 10 percent.

     Example: Your bill is $148.00. Round it up to $150.00.

     10 percent is $15.00.

     20 percent is 2 x $15 = $30.00 for the tip.

     (Of course, you can adjust the amount up or down.)

- In your head, add or subtract serial numbers (2s, 3s, 4s, etc.) from 100 as quickly as possible. Then choose a number to multiply by itself. Start with smaller numbers like 2s, 3s, and 4s to warm up, then progress to 7s, 8s, and 9s. Repeat the series daily until you can do it quickly. Then move to a new series.

2

What Can Happen to Your Brain?

IT'S A FACT: Thirty thousand neurons can fit on the head of a pin. Your brain has about one hundred billion neurons.[1]

> I like nonsense; it wakes up the brain cells.
> Dr. Seuss, referring to *The Cat in the Hat*

> You have brains in your head and feet in your shoes, you can steer yourself in any direction you choose.
> Dr. Seuss, *Oh, the Places You'll Go*

It's All in Your Head!

- Your brain weighs approximately three pounds and is about 75 percent water.
- Each neuron may be linked to another ten thousand neurons, which pass signals to each other by one thousand trillion synaptic connections.[2]

34

- The speed of nerve impulses varies in different types of neurons. The fastest can travel up to 250 mph.[3]

Those of you in the first half of your life have a big advantage over the rest of us. You're in the position of building a healthy brain instead of rebuilding a declining one. You can be setting up your brain for a lifelong trajectory of high performance.

Your active lifestyle and challenging career development provide the quality of mental exercise that's needed to keep your brain fit. Everything you do that involves variety, a challenge, or something new stimulates your memory capacity and cognitive reserve. If you're older, don't be discouraged. You have plenty of options for improvement.

Debunking Common Myths about the Brain

New research is correcting a few popular misbeliefs.[4]

- Some literature and advertisements still claim that *we use only 10 percent of our brain*. This is untrue. Actually, almost every part of the brain is active most of the time.
- *It's all downhill after age thirty*. It's true that some cognitive skills decline as we age, but some actually improve such as wisdom, vocabulary, managing emotions, better perspective, patience, and knowing our life's purpose.
- There's a history of likening the brain to the most advanced technology. The most common is that *the*

brain is like a computer: its processing speed, storage capacity, parallel circuits, inputs, and outputs. But the metaphor is a poor comparison. The brain is not hardwired like a computer. It doesn't have a set memory capacity that's waiting to be filled up, and it doesn't perform computations the way a computer does. We actively interpret, anticipate, and pay attention to different elements of the world. The brain is actually quite "moldable" (brain plasticity is the process in which the brain's neural synapses and pathways are altered as an effect of environmental, behavioral, and neural changes), unlike a computer.

- *Sneezing kills brain cells.* It doesn't.
- *Normal aging kills brain cells.* For years, it was believed that brain cells start dying around age thirty. But recent studies have determined that brain cells actually continue to develop in certain parts of the brain.[5] However, just like the rest of the body they do undergo changes because of adapting to new experiences. Age may cause a decreased number of synapses between cells. There may also be changes that disable some chemicals that communicate between cells. Neurodegenerative diseases like Alzheimer's do kill brain cells, but normal aging doesn't cause a downhill spiral.[6] It's comforting to know that some of our brain cells aren't disappearing with every birthday. They won't quit on us if we do everything we can to care for them.
- *Some of us are predominately right-brained and others are more left-brained.* This concept might have come

from Roger Sperry's studies[7] in 1967 that some functions of the left and right cerebral hemispheres are different. He concluded that the left brain is more logical, analytical, and mathematical; and the right brain is more focused on intuition, creativity, sensory input, and synthesis of information.

The speculation was that many scientists, physicians, and accountants are left-brained, while artists and composers are probably right-brained. In current research, conclusions are more complex. The evidence from more than one thousand brain scans shows no actual signs of consistent left or right dominance.[8] The key is the way the parts interact, not each part by itself. We need to work on developing both sides of our brains.

- *Listening to classical music (the "Mozart effect") makes babies smarter.*[9] It's been proven this is not the case.
- *We need to drink a lot of water to make our brains function better.* While this is not true, drinking water does help maintain the balance of body fluids, which benefits digestion, absorption, circulation, maintenance of body temperature, and transporting nutrients. (The adult human body overall is composed of about 60 percent water.)

Mental Health Matters

Nobody feels focused and mentally sharp all the time.

Mental health matters to you, me, and everyone else in the world. It's important at every stage of life, from childhood through old age. It involves our emotional, psychological, spiritual, and social well-being, and how we use our abilities and fulfill our potential. It affects how we think, feel, and act. It helps determine how we handle life's normal stresses, relate to others, and make choices.

About one in four Americans is affected by a mental illness sometime during their lifetime. Mental illness can alter thinking, mood, and behaviors, and it absolutely impairs daily functioning. Currently, depression is the most common type of mental illness.

Many factors contribute to mental health problems, but the most common are life experiences such as trauma or abuse, a family history of mental health problems, or biological factors such as an imbalance in brain chemistry.

Have you or a family member experienced a mental health problem? If not, watch for early signs of a mental illness. Being aware of and sharing information help break down the stigma and discrimination of mental illness and help others know they aren't alone in their feelings and symptoms. There are many effective resources to heal or abate the symptoms.

During the many years I practiced psychiatry at my clinic and numerous hospitals, I witnessed thousands of people struggling with mental health issues. Their amazingly complex brains were chemically off balance or damaged in other ways. Their productive lives were in danger.

Just in the past twenty years, neuroscientists have been making great strides in understanding how the brain works and discovering new technology to diagnose dysfunctions. The breakthroughs are leading to better medical treatments and hope for solving mental illness in the future.

"My Brain Is Experiencing Technical Difficulties. Please Stand By."

We fear losing cognitive function. Cognitive disorders primarily affect learning, memory, perception, and problem solving. As a society, we're twice as fearful of losing our mental capacity as having diminished physical ability. Sixty percent of adults are "very or somewhat worried" about memory loss.[10]

There are many terms used to describe the symptoms of cognitive decline, including but not limited to cognitive or memory impairment, dementia, and senility. While each has subtle differences, I'm addressing all of them together to simplify the concept of cognitive decline.

Some decline is a normal part of growing old. However, consistent or increasing problems with mental performance may suggest *cognitive impairment*. This causes changes that are serious enough to be noticed by the individuals experiencing them and/or by other people. In the mild form, changes aren't severe enough to interfere with daily life or independent function. A person with progressing cognitive or memory impairment has trouble remembering, learning new things, recalling previously learned information, concentrating, or making decisions that affect their everyday life.

Cognitive impairment can range from mild to severe. With mild impairment, people may notice changes in remembering things but are still able to do everyday activities. Conversely, severe impairment can lead to inability to understand the meaning or importance of something and inability to talk and live independently. More than sixteen million people in the United States are living with cognitive impairment.[11] There is a risk of this eventually becoming Alzheimer's or another type of dementia. However, not all people with mild cognitive impairment get worse, and some actually get better.[12]

Up to 50 percent of people over age sixty-five complain of *early cognitive decline*.[13] This shows up as a decreased ability to find the right words, remember names, concentrate, or locate objects. *Age-associated memory impairment* is common in the elderly. Many do not progress to Alzheimer's dementia, but early detection with treatment measures is essential to deter the progression.

Be Aware of Early Warning Signs

A person experiencing cognitive decline may have trouble with some of the following symptoms. Do you notice any of these in yourself, a family member, or a close friend?

- forget things more often
- forget appointments or social events
- lose your train of thought in conversations
- feel increasingly overwhelmed by making decisions, planning tasks, or following instructions
- have trouble finding your way around familiar environments
- act impulsively or show increasingly poor judgment
- have trouble learning new information

Potential Impacts of Cognitive Decline

- difficulty functioning independently and avoiding injury
- reduced awareness and ability to communicate needs
- reduced memory, judgment, and ability to exchange routine information
- difficulty performing personal management activities (i.e., paying bills)
- trouble anticipating potential consequences and problem solving
- reduced social communication skills and ability to manage emotions
- difficulty managing a home or maintaining a job or business

Dementia Is a Combination of Cognitive Deficits

Basically, dementia impacts how a person functions, understands, and acts. It's the gradual and permanent loss of brain function that occurs with certain diseases. Prevalence statistics vary, but generally about 15 percent of people older than seventy years of age have some degree of dementia.[14]

Dementia is a combination of several cognitive deficits and symptoms including decreased abilities in decision making, attention, judgment, perception, reasoning, and spatial perceptions. The chronic symptoms can be mild at first but become more severe as it progresses. Common types are Alzheimer's dementia and multi-infarct dementia. Multi-infarct dementia is also called vascular dementia and is caused by a series of small strokes over a long period. Incidentally, up to 40 percent of people with dementia may also have depression.[15] (See appendix B for all the other types of dementia.)

The good news is that some types of dementia caused by medical issues are reversible. "I'm toxic and deficient" is the mnemonic for these types:

I = infections

m = metabolic disease

t = toxins

d = nutrient deficiencies

Alzheimer's Dementia Is the Most Common Type

Sixty to 80 percent of all dementia cases are due to Alzheimer's. More than 50 percent of the population may have some dementia by age eighty-five.[16] Because people are now living longer, this is becoming a health-care emergency. The chances of developing Alzheimer's increase with age; 95 percent of the cases occur after age sixty-five. The cause of Alzheimer's is not known. Scientists believe that for most people, Alzheimer's disease is caused by a combination of genetic, lifestyle, and epigenetic risk factors that affect the brain over time. (Epigenetics are variations caused by external or environmental factors that switch genes on and off.) Besides age, other risk factors include a positive family history, history of head trauma, Down syndrome, and a heart disease history. The average survival rate is eight years after diagnosis but can span between four and twenty years. Survival may be modified significantly by interventions.

Some of the early symptoms include low energy or enthusiasm, disengagement, passivity, decreased affection, emotional lability; being unreasonable, self-centered, resistant, disinhibited; having delusions (30–50 percent), tearfulness, feelings of worthlessness, anxiety (40 percent), aggressiveness, pacing, apathy, or sleep interruptions.

More severe symptoms include the three A's—aphasia, apraxia, and agnosia.

aphasia—without words (language disturbance)
apraxia—without ability in movement (inability to carry out motor activities despite intact motor function)
agnosia—without recognition of objects

As the dementia progresses, the symptoms become more severe. But help is on the way! There are numerous drugs in development.

Sample Questions for a Cognitive Functioning Rating Report

Caregivers can help medical personnel by tracking the patient's history of dementia symptoms. It's important to document information about the timing of onset, the course of progression, and prior evaluations.

Place a check mark under the appropriate level of severity, and add notes as needed.

	None	Moderate	Severe
1. difficulty finding words	___	___	___
2. change in personality	___	___	___
3. uncooperative	___	___	___
4. aggressive/combative	___	___	___
5. talks less	___	___	___
6. smiles less	___	___	___
7. change in regular behaviors	___	___	___
8. unaware of current situation	___	___	___
Trouble with . . .			
9. recalling four words after two minutes	___	___	___
10. decreased memory (state examples)	___	___	___
11. telling time	___	___	___
12. remembering new information	___	___	___
13. hygiene/grooming	___	___	___
14. dressing/proper attire	___	___	___
15. walking, stability	___	___	___
16. bathing	___	___	___
17. eating	___	___	___
18. toileting (urinary and/or fecal incontinence)	___	___	___
19. remembering medications	___	___	___
20. remembering appointments or events	___	___	___
21. handling business affairs	___	___	___
22. paying bills	___	___	___
23. shopping	___	___	___
24. community/church/club activities	___	___	___
25. hobbies	___	___	___
26. preparing a meal	___	___	___
27. making coffee	___	___	___
28. driving	___	___	___
29. recognizing family members	___	___	___
30. recognizing acquaintances	___	___	___
31. understanding reading materials	___	___	___
32. paying attention to TV/movies	___	___	___

Consider sharing your answers to this assessment with a primary care physician for possible follow-up. It may need to be repeated every year to track changes or trends.

Dementias are the result of a combination of risk factors and complex genetic interactions. We can't change our age, family history, and heredity, but we can influence other risk factors by choosing healthy lifestyles and managing medical conditions. Some of the same guidelines for keeping your body fit may also help to keep your brain fit.

The second half of this book gives detailed recommendations for preventive mental health care. Some are common sense and things you may already be doing such as exercising, eating a healthy diet, getting enough sleep, maintaining a healthy weight, avoiding smoking and excess alcohol, decreasing stress, staying socially active, getting annual physical exams, and taking a multivitamin with antioxidants. But there are many more tools you need to consider for protecting and developing your brain fitness.

Choose Well

Our Brains Like Order and Lists

Order guides our personal, social, and professional lives. Rules, systems, networks, customs, and values guide our behaviors. We even use order in our attire, sports, dining, daily routines, and relationships.

But this sense of order can sometimes get off balance due to circumstances or medical conditions. For example, if a person is confined and deprived of normal sights and sounds for an extended time, the brain and emotions can get distorted. In loneliness, people may give inanimate objects human-like qualities. When the brain feels disorder in stressful situations, it may distort memories or reasoning, which harms relationships, productivity, emotions, and thinking. The elderly and chronically ill are particularly susceptible to these complications.

Our brains also like *lists* because information is organized and condensed, and they make immediate understanding and later recall easier. We're naturally drawn to lists because of our natural human tendency to categorize things. Our minds are used to lists because we use them in our everyday lives; even the one billion websites in our current reach are based on list formats.

Notice that I've included many lists throughout this book because lists are the best way to package a lot of information so it can be processed efficiently and retained by the brain. Choices can be made quickly by scanning the list and stopping on items that catch our attention.

I encourage you to make lists. (Here I go again . . .) Lists can help you

- remember things
- bring order to your life
- simplify and clarify
- focus
- relieve stress
- avoid procrastinating

Use them. Review them. Update them. Let them guide you.

Mind Snatchers

I saw a science fiction movie in the late 1950s called *Invasion of the Body Snatchers*. It was about a small-town doctor who discovered that the people in his community were being invaded by emotionless alien duplicates. Their bodies looked the same, but the people no longer had the same look in their eyes. Their bodies had been snatched away from their personhood.

Every day in my psychiatric practice I see middle-aged and elderly people whose minds are being snatched. They are there, but the look in their eyes says they are leaving. They either have early cognitive decline or some form of dementia. Some younger people on drugs or with other psychiatric disorders have that same look.

At the first sign of danger of a mind being snatched, action needs to be taken. The mind and memory are who a person is. The earlier the detection, the more hope there is for helpful treatment. Preventive action is especially wise considering that one person in the United States develops some form of early cognitive decline or dementia every minute.[17] Take action to reduce your risk of mental decline before it's too late.

Brain Boosters

Historical Characters

What were these people known for in history? Are all the following associations correct?

Even one wrong fact (date, association) renders the entire statement false.

		True	False
Socrates (470–399 BC)	wisdom	___	___
Cleopatra (69–30 BC)	beauty	___	___
Caligula, Roman Emperor (AD 12–41)	depravity	___	___
Attila the Hun (died in AD 453)	"the scourge of God"	___	___
Oliver Cromwell (1599–1658)	purity	___	___
Peter the Great of Russia (1672–1725)	large stature	___	___
Elizabeth the Great of Russia (1709–62)	promiscuity	___	___
Napoleon (1769–1821)	small stature	___	___
Abraham Lincoln (1809–65)	honesty	___	___
Martin Luther King Jr. (1929–68)	civil rights	___	___

History of Ideas

This historical research deals with the expression, preservation, and change of human ideas over time. It may involve the histories of philosophy, science, or literature.

Is the following sequence of ideas in correct chronological order? True or false? Some dates are approximations.

c. 3200 BC	Earliest system of writing, the cuneiform alphabet, was formed.
c. 2000 BC	Mathematics started.
507 BC	Democracy began in Athens, Greece.
AD 321	Emperor Constantine changed the Roman week to seven days, and Sunday became an official day of rest.
300–700	Gunpowder was developed by the Chinese.

1215	The jury system was developed in King John's England (Magna Carta).
c. 1400	Gutenberg developed the printing press.
c. 1540	Copernicus published the concept of the earth revolving around the sun every twenty-four hours.
c. 1663	Otto von Guericke developed the electrostatic generator.
1687	Isaac Newton developed the gravity concept of the physical universe.
c. 1740	John Harrison developed the concept of longitude, helping navigators.
1760	Industrial Revolution gained momentum.
1792	Mary Wollstonecraft's *A Vindication of the Rights of Women* was published.
1837–39	Photography was invented by Daguerre and Talbot.
1848	Karl Marx described socialism in the *Communist Manifesto*.
c. 1860	Louis Pasteur proved the relationship between germs and diseases.
1856–65	Gregor Mendes discovered genetic inheritance.
1903	The Wright brothers operated a flying machine at Kitty Hawk, North Carolina.
1905	Einstein's Theory of Special Relativity, his equation $E=MC^2$, and thoughts that preceded the atomic bomb were delivered.
1913	Henry Ford's first assembly line started.
1941	World War II, Fascism, Hitler, and Japan exerted influence and power at Pearl Harbor.
1947	Television invaded living rooms in the USA.
1936	Electronic computers started with Alan Turing, founder of modern computing.
1975	Animal rights grew with Peter Singer's *Animal Liberation*.

1984	The search for extraterrestrial intelligence was launched.
1989	The World Wide Web was started by Sir Tim Berners-Lee.
2005	Eris was discovered, 27 percent larger than Pluto and ninth largest body to orbit the sun.
2010	An aging gene was discovered that may make it possible to increase life spans and delay certain degenerative diseases.

True (correct) _____   False (incorrect) _____

Abstract Puzzle

Are you able to interpret the following mental puzzle? If not, don't feel bad—few can. Solving it takes deeper thinking than many readily attain on a daily basis.

A traveler is on her way to Delhi when she comes to a fork in the road. She is wondering which way to go when two men appear. One cannot tell the truth, and the other cannot tell a lie. The traveler doesn't know which is which. What *one* question can she ask which will show her the right road to Delhi?[18]

3

Your Aging Brain

IT'S A FACT: About 40 percent of people over age sixty-five experience some degree of memory loss.[1]

Happy Birthday! Welcome to your thirties, forties, and fifties. The years seem to pass faster and thinking seems to get slower. Are you noticing changes in decision making, multitasking, reasoning, spatial abilities, and verbal fluency? Mental fitness is a great gift to give yourself.

"Code Blue," the hospital public address system warned. The year was 1970, and I was in medical school. The announcement meant there was a medical emergency. There is a medical emergency in our health-care system today. The emergency is dementia. According to a 2013 Census Bureau report, people age sixty-five and older now make up 14 percent of America's population, totaling over forty-four million people.[2]

It's estimated that 5.2 million Americans (one in eight people) over age sixty-five have Alzheimer's disease. For people over eighty-five years, that statistic rises to the alarming rate of over 50 percent. Millions more have the forerunner of early cognitive decline, and almost 5 percent of these people will progress to Alzheimer's disease every year.[3] Death usually comes within ten years.

These projections point to disaster due to the sheer cost of these patients' medical care in the years to come. This is not to mention the families' agony that compounds the matter. What can be done? I suggest two starting points.

First, we need intense research on medications. There are over sixty drugs in testing for Alzheimer's disease. However, this has not gone so well to date. The few drugs currently approved by the US Food and Drug Administration (FDA)— Aricept, Exelon, Razadyne, Namenda, and Vayacog—only help mask the symptoms. They don't treat the underlying disease or resolve its progression.

A breakthrough Alzheimer's drug would treat the underlying disease and stop or delay the cell damage that eventually leads to the worsening of symptoms. There are several promising drugs in development and testing, but more volunteers are needed to complete clinical trials of those drugs. We also need increased federal funding of research to ensure that new ideas continue to fill the pipeline.[4]

Second, I strongly encourage everyone to start protecting your brain health now, whatever your age. The earlier you start, the better the outcome. It's never too late, even for the elderly. It's an investment in the quality of your future life.

"Code Blue." Let's go.

How Many More Years Will You Be Working?

If you are age thirty, you may be in the workforce at least thirty-seven more years before retirement. Traditionally, Social Security's full benefit retirement age was sixty-five, with early retirement available at age sixty-two. The full benefit age is now sixty-six for people born in 1943 to 1954, and it gradually rises to age sixty-seven for those born in 1960 and after. The retirement age could eventually be pushed even further, meaning more years in the workforce for today's young adults.

It's more important than ever that adults of all ages stay in the learning-and-brain-development mode as their career demands and economic pressures keep accelerating. This is more than just another responsibility added to your already busy life.

Brain fitness is the foundation, the key to success, for everything you do. For example, more people are finding or negotiating work-at-home jobs. Telecommuting and home-based careers are becoming more plentiful as corporate cultures are reengineered and technology expands. Employees enjoy the flexible schedules, convenience, no commuting, and home office tax deductions. But there are stressors too. The frequent transitions between employee and family roles, limited socialization, and lack of collaboration with colleagues are just a few. To be successful, home workers need to stay motivated, self-disciplined, focused, and mentally sharp.

But no matter where you work or how old you are, the goal is to function at your peak mental performance for as long as you can.

Aging Is Highly Individualized

Millions of baby boomers (those born after World War II between 1946 and 1964) are reaching the Social Security age. These people are now between fifty-two and seventy years old. Census projections estimate that by 2020 this group will make up over 16 percent of America's total population.[5]

But it's not just baby boomers who have the aging process on their minds. Young adults and middle-aged people are stressing over their future physical and mental capabilities because of the prominent media coverage of aging issues and the many antiaging retail products. The fitness, memory games, and diet industries are jumping on the bandwagon. This is great for bringing awareness to the importance of preserving health, but it doesn't do any good unless each individual gets on the bandwagon and takes action.

The way people age is very individualized. The number of years lived is not always the best measure of health. Birthdays come every 365 days, but biological (functional) age can vary greatly because of the complexity of the aging process. Our minds and bodies are influenced by a variety of experiences, medical conditions, genetic factors, long-term lifestyle factors, and even by cultural differences.

For example, it's been proven that biological age can be lowered by regular mental and physical exercise and by maintaining a healthy lifestyle. A Harvard University study reported that people who walk an average of just eleven minutes a day live almost two years longer than those who don't exercise at all.[6]

Brace Yourself for the Aging Process

In some cases, the normal physical and mental changes involved in aging may be even more dramatic if underlying medical conditions are not well managed or if adequate nutrition, sleep, exercise, and social interactions are lacking. But generally, the following list describes typical symptoms of aging. By taking care of yourself, you may be able to delay or avoid at least some of these issues.

Stay alert for changes that could develop into chronic problems, and develop good habits that can head off problems. It's also important to establish a good relationship with a primary care doctor for preventive checkups and care.

- Normal aging involves *biological changes* in the central nervous system, brain cells, and body chemicals.
- *Neurological changes*—the gradual decline in the blood flow to the brain—can affect metabolism, sleep patterns, and parts of the nervous system. They may eventually slow reflexes and affect balance. The brain doesn't send or process nerve impulses as well or as quickly. Mental changes happen at different rates and intensities for each person. Some brain functions may remain stable while other functions decline.
- It gets harder to lose weight, and skin loses elasticity. Joints, muscles, teeth, blood circulation, digestion, and immune systems begin to show their age.
- *Physical activities* decline with the loss of muscle strength, muscle mass, and flexibility. Some motor

dysfunctions may predict a later onset of Alzheimer's and cognitive decline.

- Less air is taken in with each breath, and the *lungs* don't absorb as much oxygen.

- The *senses* aren't spared either. Age-related dry mouth, dry eyes, and hearing loss are common. The eyes react more slowly to changes in light, and glaucoma and cataracts develop. High-pitched sounds are particularly hard for the elderly to hear.

- *Eating problems* result from less sensitive taste buds, decreased sense of smell, and difficulty chewing and swallowing.

- More noticeably, *good looks* are lost. Hair thins and turns gray, dry skin wrinkles and heals more slowly, and body fat gets redistributed.

- There is a general decline in the function of *internal organs and systems* and an increase in illnesses such as diabetes, heart disease, hypertension, and cancer.

- Testosterone and estrogen *hormone levels* also diminish, which can produce age-related sexual dysfunction.

- *Stress* affects the quality of relationships. Losses, fears, and boredom increase.

- *Energy levels* depend more on lifestyle and attitude than chronological age. Good nutrition, restful sleep, and regular exercise can help keep energy levels high.

- With advancing age, *psychological problems* can set in. There is often a decline in self-esteem because of dependency and a narrowing of interests. Friendships can fade when unhealthy coping defenses surface, such as withdrawing and giving up.

- *Depression* is the most common mental disorder in the vulnerable elderly. Typical symptoms include sadness, health-related and bodily function worries, sleep disturbance, loss of appetite, low energy, and back pain. Emotions are easily triggered, and judgment is compromised.

But all of this doesn't mean you have to give up or be cranky in your senior years. Happiness is a choice just like preserving your memory is a choice. You can make every stage of life fulfilling, peaceful, and productive if you choose. It's encouraging to know that Benjamin Franklin, Albert Schweitzer, Winston Churchill, and Michelangelo made their major contributions in their eighties.

Abraham Lincoln said it well: "Most people are about as happy as they choose to be." Some studies have determined that happiness may decline in the first few decades of adulthood, but it often upswings again later. Life satisfaction typically dips when people are in their forties and then increases as they reach their sixties, which is good news for seniors. A 2011 study from Stanford University concluded that peak emotional life may not actually occur until the seventh decade.[7] An anonymous individual testifies to this:

There is great freedom that comes with aging. I know I'm sometimes forgetful. But some of life is just as well forgotten. Eventually, I remember the important things. I am so blessed to have lived long enough to have my youthful laughs etched into grooves on my face. As you get older, it is easier to be positive. You care less about what other people think. I like being old.[8]

How Are Dementia and Alzheimer's Disease Different?

Dementia and Alzheimer's disease are often used interchangeably, which is confusing for patients, families, and caregivers. Everyone occasionally forgets things or has difficulty finding words. This is normal and doesn't mean it will progress into either dementia or Alzheimer's disease.

But it's important to recognize when simple forgetfulness develops into something more serious. See a physician if you or a loved one begins to decline in other ways. It's often a medical disorder, not aging, that accounts for loss of motor, physical, or psychological functions.

Dementia is the general term associated with cognitive decline, often related to aging. It's used for symptoms that may include impaired memory and thinking, disturbance in planning and organizing, inability to carry out motor activities, and information and language disturbance.

Early warning signs of dementia may be forgetting how to perform basic tasks such as making change from a dollar bill, forgetting where the keys are kept, or neglecting hygiene or safety precautions—memory loss that disrupts daily life. These signs threaten a person's social and occupational life and warrant a trip to a doctor.

Common causes of dementia are Alzheimer's disease, Huntington's disease, Parkinson's disease, Creutzfeldt-Jakob disease; traumatic brain injury, TIAs (transient ischemic attacks), endocrine disorders, chronic subdural hematoma, infections (HIV), and toxins (long-term drug or alcohol use).[9] Some forms of dementia caused by drug interactions or vitamin deficiencies may be temporary or reversible. Once a cause of dementia is determined, appropriate treatments can begin.

Alzheimer's disease is the most common cause of dementia among older adults. It's a form of dementia that specifically affects parts of the brain that control thought, memory, and language. Learning ability decreases as well as the recall of recent events and knowledge. Alzheimer's is not a reversible condition. It is degenerative and incurable at this time.

In stage 1, there may be no obvious symptoms except for early cognitive decline. About 20 percent of early cognitive decline patients will progress to Alzheimer's disease each year. If the Alzheimer's brain pathology is present, the disease progresses.

Some of the difficult changes in stage 2 are swings in behaviors and mood. Medical issues and drug interactions may compound these problems. Patients may have emotional outbursts, going from calm to tears to anger for no apparent reason. Their personalities may change, and many become confused, fearful or anxious, agitated, argumentative, disinhibited, aggressive, or even delusional (30–50 percent). Patients may also be apathetic, disengaged, or have poor sleep, decreased affection, and repetition of actions and speech.[10]

As this form of dementia progresses to stage 3, the symptoms become more severe. It becomes more difficult to find words (aphasia); recognize objects (agnosia); and carry out motor activities despite intact motor function (apraxia). There is also a significant decrease in reasoning, judgment, problem solving, and the ability to learn and retain information. Eventually, vocabulary is only about one to six intelligible words, and patients can no longer walk, sit up, or hold up their heads.[11]

The brain changes in Alzheimer's can begin up to twenty years before the actual onset. The physiological changes involve diffuse atrophy of the brain cells, increased senile plaques, increased neurofibrillary tangles, increased amyloid proteins, and enlarged cerebral ventricles. Acetylcholine is the neurotransmitter of the brain most affected in Alzheimer's. This chemical plays a role in the signals for muscle movement, learning, memory formation, and some regulation of the endocrine system.

Doctors use a variety of screenings to determine the cause and levels of dementia. The most common tools include mental status evaluations with cognitive measurements; brain scans—MRI (magnetic resonance imaging) and PET (positron emission tomography) imaging to measure Alzheimer's biomarkers, atrophy, plaques, and sensitivities; and blood tests involving genotype markers and biomarkers in CSF (cerebrospinal fluid).[12]

Risk Factors for Alzheimer's

There is evidence that the following factors may *increase the risk* of developing Alzheimer's:

- increasing age is the greatest-known risk factor
- family history—genetics: how the genes we are born with are expressed depends partially on long-term lifestyle and other factors. These can have an effect

on whether certain genes are turned on or off. Alzheimer's has a genetic factor, but it doesn't always result in disease onset.

- consistently high cholesterol and blood pressure
- midlife obesity
- diabetes mellitus or chronic kidney disease with increased serum creatinine
- long-term psychological stress or depression
- smoking and exposure to environmental toxins (fertilizers, pesticides, fumigants, defoliants)
- head injury, especially if it involved a loss of consciousness or frequent, repeated trauma
- presence of other diseases
- having the APOE4 genotype, increased homocysteine (amino acid), increased amyloid and phosphorylated tau in spinal fluid, which are Alzheimer's biomarkers
- Down syndrome
- low level of education
- prior damage to the heart or blood vessels (strokes, high blood pressure, high cholesterol)

Some of these risk factors can't be changed or influenced, such as age and family genes. But many factors are in our control, such as maintaining a healthy lifestyle and making such wellness choices as managing underlying medical conditions. These can impact the risks as well as the outcome.

On the other hand, the following factors may *decrease the risk* of developing Alzheimer's:

- mental exercise, which increases brain dendrites and neuroplasticity (the brain's ability to reorganize itself by forming new neural connections), and neurogenesis (birth and growth of neurons/nerve cells)
- physical exercise to get more oxygen to the brain
- antioxidants (omega-3 fatty acids; vitamins C, E, B_6, B_9, B_{12}; curry)
- stop smoking (nicotine) and drinking alcohol in excess
- control blood pressure and cholesterol levels
- decrease long-term stress and consider an antidepressant if needed
- maintain a healthy diet including natural foods
- lose excess weight
- consult a medical doctor for regular checkups
- stay socially connected
- increase education and reading
- reduce stress and anxiety by staying focused on what's important and shrug off the rest
- caffeine may possibly help
- NSAIDs (anti-inflammatories) are still in debate. The NSAIDs that can decrease the Alzheimer's AB42 biomarker are ibuprofen, indomethacin, and Clinoril.[13]

Tips for Caring for Someone with Dementia

Caring for a dementia patient is certainly challenging for families and caregivers. The goal is to try to make every day as easy as possible for everyone involved. Mid- to late-stage dementia is the most challenging time. The fear, anger, sadness, confusion, and paranoia the person is experiencing can result in oppositional and aggressive speech and actions.

Communication can be one of the most challenging aspects of patient care. Make adjustments to reduce the stress and to manage difficult behaviors:[14]

- speak slowly and simply, and in a normal volume (a raised voice will increase tension and agitation)
- use a calm and soothing tone of voice and open body language
- point and gesture to clarify directions and requests
- rephrase requests as needed, giving the person a moment to process the request
- use only one command or direction at a time
- don't argue or take offense
- don't interrupt, criticize, or correct
- show respect by avoiding baby talk
- watch what you say; assume the person can understand what you are saying

Some activities can be therapeutic:
- read and play memory games
- do crosswords and puzzles

- socialize with friends
- use the opposite hand for routine tasks to stimulate the brain and hand-eye coordination
- sing old songs from the past
- get daily physical exercise
- emphasize word memorization for as long as possible
- encourage the sharing of favorite memories daily
- reduce (or even better, eliminate) distractions such as TV or radio; too much noise can be overstimulating and upsetting

Maintain a safe environment:

- install safety latches high on doors
- limit choices to avoid confusion
- remove tripping/fall hazards (footstools, magazine racks, loose rugs)
- keep closets and drawers uncluttered (necessities only)
- install gates at the top and bottom of stairs
- place colored strips to mark steps, entrances, and exits
- fence off pools and outdoor hazards
- use night-lights and motion-sensor lights around the house
- remove firearms
- lower the temperature on the water heater

- get an alarm system to alert for open doors or windows

Insights to support caregivers as well as patients:

- emphasize pleasant memories from the past
- keep a predictable routine and structured environment
- give reassurance and be patient
- don't challenge anger; attempt to switch focus to a new activity
- ignore offensive language and try to redirect
- be aware that patients don't like to be touched when they are agitated
- stay calm; try not to take poor behavior personally
- focus on the patient and not on the specific task
- stay flexible because capacities to perform daily functions such as going to the bathroom and eating and sleeping can differ from day to day
- follow the Alzheimer's Association's three-step process to manage difficult behaviors: identify the behavior, understand the cause, and then adapt[15]

Some of you may already have confronted some of the realities of aging. You've probably noticed some of them in the mirror and others in the aches and pains that linger a little longer after yard work or exercise.

I encourage you to stay positive and focus on your blessings. Be smart about taking care of yourself and keep your sense of humor.

Choose Well

I hope you are becoming more convinced of the importance of protecting your brain from cognitive decline. There are many tips and guidelines in the second half of this book to help you plan a personalized brain-care action plan.[16]

An ounce of prevention is worth a pound of cure.

Benjamin Franklin, statesman and scientist

Prevention is a whole lot less costly than treatment and maybe more effective.

Debbie Adair, author

The doctor of the future will give no medicine but will interest his patients in the care of the human frame in diet and in the cause and prevention of disease.

Thomas A. Edison, inventor

America's health-care system is in crisis precisely because we systematically neglect wellness and prevention.

Tom Harkin, politician

Prevention is one of the few known ways to reduce demand for health- and aged-care services.

Julie Bishop, politician

As a practicing neurologist, I place central importance in applying current science to the notion of prevention.

David Perlmutter, physician

Preventive care is your healthcare practice that you participate in every day of your life.

truewellnessgroup.com

Preventive care is about healthy lifestyle habits with no end date in sight. Start today; your body will thank you by staying strong and healthy.

Katie Jodscheidt, Innerzyme.com

Unless someone like you cares a whole awful lot, nothing is going to get better. It's not.

Dr. Seuss, *The Lorax*

Do not regret growing older. It's a privilege denied to many.

Unknown

Brain Boosters

United States Government

The government of the United States is the federal government of the republic of fifty states, as well as one capital district and several territories. The full name of the republic is United States of America. No other name appears in the Constitution.

Are all of the following statements correct? (All of the details must be accurate for a true rating.)

	True	False
1. The number of US senators is 100.		
2. The number of US representatives is 435.		
3. The number of Supreme Court justices is 9.		
4. United States senators serve unlimited six-year terms.		
United States representatives serve unlimited two-year terms.		
5. The amendment to the US Constitution that gave women the right to vote was the Nineteenth Amendment.		
6. The three branches of government are executive (president and fifteen departments), judicial (courts), and legislative (Senate and House of Representatives).		
7. Medicare started in 1965.		
8. The national government cannot change state boundaries.		
9. Congress can override the president's veto of a bill.		
10. A probate court is for matters involving wills, estates, and guardianship of children.		

United States Constitution

The Preamble to the US Constitution states:

We the People of the United States, in Order to form a more perfect Union, establish Justice, insure domestic Tranquility, provide for the common defense, promote the general Welfare, and secure the Blessings of Liberty to ourselves and our Posterity, do ordain and establish this Constitution for the United States of America.

Are the following statements correct? (All of the details must be accurate for a true rating.)

Amendment	True	False
1. freedom of speech, religion, assembly, and press	___	___
2. right to bear arms	___	___
4. prohibits unreasonable search and seizure	___	___
5. right to due process; no testifying against self	___	___
6. right to fair, speedy, public trial	___	___
7. right to jury trial	___	___
8. prohibits cruel or excessive punishment	___	___
10. limits powers of federal government	___	___
13. abolishes slavery	___	___
14. defines citizenship	___	___
15. prohibits denial of the right to vote based on race, color, or previous condition of servitude	___	___
16. allows federal government to collect income tax	___	___
19. women's right to vote	___	___
26. voting age eighteen years	___	___

4

Stress and Your Brain

IT'S A FACT: Chronic, excessive stress can alter our brain cells and our brain structure and function.

Stress comes from external situations (pointing outward) as a response to life's pressures.

"I'm so stressed I feel like I'm silently screaming! I can't keep up with everything at home and work, and I'm always exhausted and don't feel good. It feels like I'm driving with no brakes. I can't relax and racing thoughts keep me up at night. I feel like a walking time bomb, and there's no end in sight."

Think about your own stress level. If this is how you feel, imagine what it's doing to your physical and mental health and especially to your relationships. Friends and family members get dragged down too. If your calendar is seriously overbooked, your kids' schedules probably are too. Bedtimes are too late, and mornings and evenings are chaotic. Be aware that the lack of sleep on a regular basis can harm the physical and mental development of children.

This kind of stress has become an accepted and normal part of daily life. Our demanding jobs, unmet obligations, trying to make ends meet financially, and illness in the family can be chronic stressors or the final straw. Some of this stress can be managed, but some can't, and this takes a toll.

We think of stress as temporary incidents, but it's more than that. It sets in when we perceive that the demands placed on us exceed our ability to perform and cope. Bouts of stress make us feel irritable, tense, and forgetful. But over time, elevated levels of cortisol, the stress hormone, chip away at our mental, emotional, and physical health.

Warning: This can trigger short- and long-term brain impairment.

Our Brains Need Us to Stop Stressing Out

When brain chemicals are in balance, we feel sharp and focused, and in downtimes we're calm and relaxed. But when they're out of balance, the brain stays in constant stress mode causing memory loss and impaired cognitive function.

The more stressed out we are, the greater the risk to our brain health. For instance, chronic stress contributes to lost volume in the medial prefrontal cortex (associated with emotional and cognitive impairment). The production of new neurons generated in the hippocampus is decreased (associated with learning, memory, and emotion). The insula (attention and focus), the amygdala (center for emotional responses and motivation), and other parts of the brain don't go unscathed.

Chronic stress can also increase sensitivity to medications. Drugs that normally affect us in one way may become more potent. And in the long term, chronic stress is linked to Alzheimer's disease and dementia. So basically, the more stress, the worse the brain performs.

It's been estimated that almost 50 percent of adults suffer from the effects of stress. It's obvious because 75–90 percent of all visits to primary health-care providers are due to stress-related problems.[1] This is a serious cultural and health-care problem, and it is discussed here in detail.

Stress Affects All Areas of Our Lives

Stress is personal. What causes stress in one person may be no big deal to another. Some people can handle certain types of stress while others fall apart.

Not all stress is bad. Our bodies are designed to handle *small doses of stress*. It can help us accomplish tasks on time and even keep us from getting hurt. For example, this boost of alertness and energy can help get us through heavy traffic or meet important deadlines at work. Small doses can be helpful.

There's another kind of stress. When we feel threatened, a chemical reaction is triggered in the body known as the *fight-or-flight stress response*. This automatic reaction causes an increase in heart and breathing rates, tightening of muscles, a rise in blood sugar and blood pressure, and an increase in the blood flow to the brain and large muscles. This surge of adrenaline puts the body on alert, ready to act. After the threat passes, the body relaxes again.

Reactions to *stress caused from normal fears* may not be quite that extreme. Fear is a feeling of uneasiness or agitation. We fear being hurt. We fear the house burning down while we're on vacation, and thrill rides at amusement parks. Alzheimer's is one of the most feared diseases. Most fears are mild and fleeting and are nothing to be concerned about because the risk passes or what is feared never comes true.

But unrealistic fears can turn into *irrational phobias*. The irony then is that fear itself brings the very pain we're trying to avoid. The symptoms of unhealthy fear can include many of the same symptoms as stress but with extra intensity. For example, there can be unpleasant sensations of smothering or numbness, hyperventilation, weakness in the legs, chills, blurred vision, and a strong sense of losing control.

Long-term, *chronic stress* is the most damaging. This happens when situations aren't temporary, such as relationship problems, loneliness, financial worries, or excessive work schedules. Our bodies aren't designed to handle persistent tension without negative consequences. It wears down our emotions, behaviors, physical health, and mental stability. No part of the body goes unscathed.

Because people handle stress differently, the causes and symptoms can also vary. Some are vague while others might cause symptoms of a medical condition. It's important to stay aware of worrisome signs of illness and changes in how you feel or act. A medical doctor can determine if you're experiencing the effects of chronic stress or have another underlying medical issue. Either way, help is needed.

Self-Assessment: Stress-Level Symptoms

Stress produces a variety of physical, psychological, mental, and behavioral symptoms. It can also trigger an illness or aggravate existing health problems.

It matters how you personally handle it. The best way is to keep track of all your symptoms. By rating the following common signs of chronic stress, you may be able to determine if it's an acceptable, manageable factor in your lifestyle or if it has become detrimental to your overall health.

The list below is not comprehensive and is not a standardized medical evaluation. It simply provides an overview of possible symptoms that may help you become more aware of your emotional and physical well-being. It's a starting point for making new choices for improving your health.

Please rate each of the symptoms on a scale of 0 to 10. This will help you assess your stress intensity levels so you can work on eliminating stressors or increasing your tolerance level.

- 0 = none
- 1, 2, or 3 = mild/minor/noticeable—annoying but doesn't interfere with daily activities
- 4, 5, or 6 = moderate/moderately strong—interferes with daily activities
- 7, 8, or 9 = disabling/intense—unable to perform daily activities
- 10 = severe

Emotional Symptoms

depression, feeling sad, crying spells ____

frequent mood swings ____

worried, upset ____

anxious, nervous, restless ____

agitation, frustration, feeling overwhelmed ____

anger, outbursts, irritability, hostility, annoyance ____

low motivation, few interests ____

trouble paying attention, distractible, forgetful ____

tense, difficulty relaxing ____

low self-esteem, lonely ____

fearful, defensive, suspicious ____

upsetting dreams ____

burnout, emotional exhaustion ____

other _____

Cognitive Symptoms

confusion, poor judgment, difficulty making
   decisions ____

forgetful, disorganized ____

unable to focus or concentrate, racing thoughts ____

difficulty communicating ____

stuttering, stammering, can't think of words ____

trouble learning new information ____

irrational worrying ____

pessimistic, focusing on negatives ____

other _____

Behavioral Symptoms

obsessive compulsions or repetitive actions ____

trouble functioning at work, at home, or socially ____

avoiding others, social withdrawal ____

procrastination, avoiding responsibilities ____

increased use of alcohol, drugs, or cigarettes ____

nervous habits: fidgeting, nail biting, pacing ____

increased addictions such as shopping, gambling ____

more minor accidents, clumsy ____

lies or has excuses to cover up actions ____

inefficient, unproductive ____

excessive or inappropriate use of over-the-counter
    drugs ____

poor grooming and hygiene, disinterest in
    appearance ____

rapid or mumbled speech ____

other _____

Physical Symptoms

insomnia, difficulty falling or staying asleep, changed
    sleeping habits, nightmares ____

jaw clenching, gritting or grinding teeth ____

faint, dizzy, light-headed ____

allergy episodes ____

muscle tension, aches, spasms, or pain ____

frequent headaches ____

heartburn, stomach pain, nausea, indigestion ____

constipation, diarrhea ____

frequent urination ____

fatigue, low energy, weakness ____

chest pain, rapid heartbeat ____

frequent colds and infections ____

loss of sexual desire and/or ability ____

dry mouth ____

panic attacks ____

shaking, trembling, twitching ____

shortness of breath, frequent sighing ____

ear ringing, popping, or buzzing ____

hot flashes, blushing, sweating ____

cold or sweaty hands, feet ____

rashes, itching, hives ____

excessive belching or flatulence ____

changes in appetite or weight ____

other _____

How Chronic Stress Affects Your Body

Stress begets more stress. Some stress every now and then is nothing to worry about. However, ongoing stress can cause or make existing health problems worse. Symptoms of many preexisting medical conditions can also worsen during times of stress. It isn't easy to completely stop the constant tension, but it can be decreased.

Chronic stress moves people out of the normal physical and mental zones. It may even trigger vulnerable genetic factors that play a role in diseases. Stress increases inflammatory cytokines (secreted by certain cells of the immune system and have an effect on other cells), which, in turn, increase autoantibodies that are directed at our own tissues.

- When inflammatory cytokines attack the *cardiovascular* (CV) *system*, a person can develop or worsen their heart conditions, including coronary and arteriosclerotic heart disease, high blood pressure, arrhythmias, angina, congestive heart failure, abnormal heart rhythms, heart attacks, and strokes.
- *Central nervous system* (CNS) diseases such as Alzheimer's and other dementias are often intensified.
- *Gastrointestinal* (GI) issues can worsen irritable bowel syndrome and be a factor in peptic ulcer disease, Crohn's disease, ulcerative colitis, gastroesophageal reflux disease (GERD), and gastritis.
- In the *respiratory system*, stress makes a person more prone to bronchitis, asthmatic attacks, chronic obstructive pulmonary disease (COPD) flare-ups, and allergic rhinitis.
- When increased inflammatory cytokines and autoantibodies attack the *immune system*, one is more likely to develop an autoimmune disease that turns the body on itself. With the increased chronic inflammation, stress triggers chemical changes that can increase the occurrence of diabetes mellitus II, hyperthyroidism, hypothyroidism, rheumatoid

arthritis, celiac disease, lupus, Crohn's disease, or Sjögren's syndrome.

- The *skin or integumentary system* becomes more prone to acne, psoriasis, eczema, infections, pruritus, psoriasis, urticaria, dermatitis, eczema, and alopecia; stress is a factor in at least 30 percent of dermatology problems.[2]

- Stress and *mental disorders* are also connected. Depression, mood and anxiety disorders, and other psychological and personality disorders are impacted by stress.

Other medical conditions affected by increased inflammatory cytokines include hypoglycemia, obesity, eating disorders, menstrual problems, and sexual dysfunctions. Patients under chronic stress are even more prone to cancer.[3]

Some people turn to cigarettes, alcohol, drugs, or other addictions, which further damage the brain and body. The goal is to learn how to better control your reaction to stress and to manage or eliminate the stressors in your control. That is a matter of choice.

Stress triggers many chemical reactions. Think about how this illustration relates to your struggle with stress. What sets you off? How do you react? Look at what it's doing to you.

What Stress Does to Your Brain

- Stress decreases the biogenic amines (neurotransmitters such as serotonin) that make you happy.

- It decreases a chemical called BDNF (brain-derived neurotrophic factor) that keeps you mentally sharp. It's been called the "Miracle-Gro for brains." Decreased BDNF results in decreased neurons. People who are depressed have lower BDNF, which plays a critical role in memory.[4]

- Stress triggers the release of the hormone cortisol. Raised levels of cortisol can trigger long-term changes in brain structure, connectivity, and function. Too much cortisol makes the brain more vulnerable to strokes, premature aging, and impaired memory. The increase in inflammatory cytokines can decrease brain function and be a factor in dementia.

Adults in Their Peak Years Are at Risk

Some adult roles are changing because of a current trend that's impacting many families across America. Grown children are moving back home, and elderly parents are living longer and needing help. Even though families are dispersed across the country, most adults are getting involved in caring for multiple generations.

The following is more than an example; it's a warning that chronic stress is threatening the brain health of many adults in their peak years.

People in the traditional "sandwich generation" are in their thirties, forties, and more recently, their fifties. They're taking care of their children as well as meeting the needs of their aging parents who are living longer and needing supervised care.

Young adults ranging from ages of twenty-five to thirty-four are becoming known as the "boomerang generation." It's more common for them to live with their parents because of economic hardships. The "sandwiched" adults are now responsible for helping two generations, in addition to taking care of themselves, with daily routines, medical services, supervision, medications, finances, and the legal and emotional needs of their loved ones. This affects the caregivers' finances, personal time, careers, and mental health. They are succumbing to stress and burnout.

The "club sandwich generation" includes those in their fifties and sixties sandwiched between aging parents, adult children, and grandchildren, or those in their thirties and forties with young children, aging parents, and grandparents. The "open-faced generation" is anyone else involved in elder care.[5]

All of these situations and relationships are different, so there are no right or wrong ways to manage the chronic stress. But here are a few ideas that may help those caught in the multigenerational maze:

- Set boundaries for financial spending for both the grown children and the elderly parents and stay within the agreed-upon budgets.
- Communicate. Regularly gather all three generations to discuss tasks, schedules, and finances. Seek outside help for unmet needs.
- Mentor children over eighteen to prepare to live independently.

- Consider having aging parents move into your home. Three generations living together is becoming a more popular trend. It saves time and money. Caregivers can claim tax benefits and medical-care reductions, and deduct the medical bills on tax returns. At least do the math.

- Take care of yourself. The needs of caregivers often get overlooked.

We Live in a Stressful World

On a broader scale, during the last one hundred years, you, your grandparents, and great-grandparents have been exposed to a series of traumatic events and major lifestyle changes. Every decade has been marked with some kind of turbulence, and the resulting stress impacts mental health.

The following examples highlight some of these life-changing or stressful events.

Economic Stability Is Always Uncertain

The American economy has experienced periods of material prosperity and devastating decline. People at all income levels are affected. In fact, your family has probably been affected by economic changes just in the last fifteen years. The average wealth in American households has declined by approximately one-third. Food, fuel, taxes, and utilities have increased as much as 100 percent.[6]

These are uncertain times; there have been others in recent history. The 1929–39 Great Depression was the deepest and longest-lasting economic downturn. It began after the stock market crash in 1929. Consumer spending and investments dropped, causing declines in industrial output, failed banks, and unemployment. The average American family income dropped by 40 percent. The stock market didn't return to pre-Depression levels until the 1950s.

The 1970 economic recession put an end to the post–World War II economic boom. It was a period of stagnation when high unemployment coincided with high inflation. Widespread unemployment continued through the recession in the late 1970s and early 1980s. Long-term effects contributed to the savings and loan crisis and new economic policies in the 1980s and 1990s.

In 2008 the world economy faced its most dangerous crisis since the 1930s. The downturn spread to the financial sector and financial markets overseas. Casualties included the investment banking industry, insurance companies, mortgage lenders, commercial banks, and the auto industry. The Dow Jones Industrial Average lost one-third of its value, and home prices dropped almost as much.

The fragile economy continues to waiver as our nation struggles with the effects of global finance, trade, and energy controversies. Closer to home, health care and immigration policies are unresolved. Cyberattacks, growing poverty levels, unemployment, and corporate failures contribute to ongoing economic instability.

Many of these issues have impacted our ancestors as well as our families today. Being good stewards of our personal resources can help us cope with current and future economic challenges.

Environmental Disasters Are Constant Threats

Earthquakes, tsunamis, typhoons, volcano eruptions, floods, blizzards, hurricanes, extreme weather patterns, and other natural disasters keep coming. Managing natural resources, adjusting to climate changes, and mitigating oil spills, fires, droughts, and pollution are growing concerns.

Emergency preparedness is a priority for all levels of government. The US Department of Homeland Security's Federal Emergency Management Agency (FEMA) encourages everyone to have emergency plans and supplies for homes, schools, and businesses.

In 2004 the Southeast Asian tsunami followed a 9.3 Richter scale earthquake in the Indian Ocean and killed 290,000 people. Hurricane Katrina was a deadly and destructive Atlantic tropical cyclone in 2005. It is the most costly natural disaster, as well as one of the five deadliest hurricanes (1,300 people perished), in the history of the United States. Hurricane Sandy in 2012 was our country's second most costly hurricane. Sandy became the largest Atlantic hurricane on record.

We've witnessed the aftermath of environmental tragedies through detailed reports and videos in news coverage, and many families have been directly affected by these stressors.

International Mobility Spreads Epidemics

Also on our minds are the risks and challenges of international travel. General safety precautions can reduce the risk of exposure to infectious illnesses and complying with required vaccinations is important.

Pandemics and epidemics have been documented throughout history. Plagues, cholera, typhus, smallpox, and influenza have devastated cultures around the world. The influenza pandemic in 1918–19 was a global disaster. Approximately 20–40 percent of the world's population became ill, and an estimated 50 million people died. Nearly 675,000 people died in the United States.[7] The 1976 swine flu outbreak was a strain of H1N1 influenza virus. Although infections were limited, the outbreak is most remembered for the mass immunization that it prompted. In 2009 the swine flu was deemed a global pandemic. According to the World Health Organization, if a new strain of influenza caused a pandemic to emerge today, we could expect a vaccine for the new strain of the virus and antibiotics to treat secondary infections to be in short supply. Medical facilities and personnel would be overwhelmed.

At its peak in the 1940s and 1950s, polio paralyzed or killed over half a million people worldwide every year. The collective fear spurred the development of new methods to prevent and treat the disease. Although the development of the polio vaccine has nearly eradicated poliomyelitis, a positive legacy remains in the development of rehabilitation therapy and the rise of disability rights movements.

In 1981 the United States was the first country to bring Human Immunodeficiency Virus (HIV) and Acquired Immunodeficiency Syndrome (AIDS) to the public consciousness. The American reaction contributed to AIDS being one of the most politicized, feared, and controversial diseases of modern medicine.

Severe Acute Respiratory Syndrome (SARS) in early 2003 spread to twenty-nine countries, killing nearly 10 percent of the people it infected. SARS also became a scourge of national economies, with costs measured in billions of dollars.[8]

The Ebola virus is a severe hemorrhagic disease that first appeared in 1976 in Sudan and the Democratic Republic of Congo. In 2014, an Ebola pandemic broke out in West Africa. According to the World Health Organization, past Ebola outbreaks have seen fatality rates up to 90 percent. The threat of the Ebola virus is new to the United States. The Center for Disease Control and Prevention (CDC) is actively promoting public awareness and health safety standards.

Violence Breeds Fear

The stress gets worse because it is infiltrating every home. Our families are exposed to violent acts every day as they watch the news and TV shows. Through intense media coverage, we witness buildings being destroyed, gunmen unleashing fire at schools and other public places, and soldiers being maimed.

The media's frequent coverage of abduction, domestic violence, robbery, and murder heightens our perception of potential violence. This is also pervasive subject matter in TV programming; it stresses us and then numbs us to its effects. Children watch so many virtual acts of violence that some begin to accept it as a way to solve problems. The virtual environment can actually change people's behavior.

Violence is also glorified in the movie industry, music videos, online gaming, internet sites, and popular books and magazines. With the average American gaming or surfing the internet several hours every day, violence and graphic images are invading our minds. There are mental health consequences.

America's involvement in wars has also impacted many families. World War I was a global war centered in Europe from 1914 to 1918. Approximately sixteen million people were killed.

World War II, 1939–45, involved more than thirty nations making up two opposing military alliances. It was the most widespread war in history and involved more than one hundred million people. The bombing of industrial and population centers resulted in an estimated fifty to eighty-five million fatalities, making it the deadliest conflict in human history.

The violence of the Holocaust was unprecedented. Between 1941 and 1945, Jews were targeted and methodically murdered in the largest genocide of the twentieth century. Approximately six million Jews were killed. This genocide was part of a broader act of oppression and killings of various ethnic and political groups in Europe by the Nazis.

The 1950–53 Korean War between North and South Korea arose from the division of Korea at the end of World War II and from the global tensions of the Cold War that developed immediately afterward. A United Nations force led by the United States fought for the South, and China fought for the North, assisted by the Soviet Union.

The Vietnam War pitted the Communist regime of North Vietnam and its southern allies, the Viet Cong, against South Vietnam and its principal ally, the United States. The war ended with the withdrawal of US forces in 1973 and the unification of Vietnam under Communist control two years later.

The September 11, 2001, terrorist attacks in New York and Washington, DC, were launched by the Islamic terrorist group al-Qaeda. Two airplanes were flown into the towers of the World Trade Center in New York City and a third plane hit the Pentagon just outside Washington, DC. A passenger plane was brought down by terrorists in a field in Pennsylvania. The attacks killed over three thousand people and caused at least $10 billion in property and infrastructure damage.

The first phase of the Iraq War was an invasion of Iraq starting in 2003 by a force led by the United States, ending Ba'athist Iraq. It was followed by a longer phase of fighting, in which an insurgency emerged to oppose the occupying forces and the newly formed Iraqi government. The United States completed its withdrawal of military personnel in 2011, during the ninth year of the war. The insurgency is ongoing and continues to cause fatalities by the thousands.

The war in Afghanistan (2001 to present) is the intervention by the North Atlantic Treaty Organization (NATO) and allied forces in the ongoing Afghan civil war. The purpose is to dismantle al-Qaeda and deny it a basis of operation in Afghanistan by removing the Taliban from power. Tens of thousands of people have been killed.

The war on terror continues. Threats to Israel and the worldwide peace process put many nations at risk. The news media continues to report activities of ISIS, the Islamic State of Iraq and Syria, and ISIL, the Islamic State of Iraq and the Levant (the undefined region around Syria including Syria, Lebanon, Israel, Palestine, and Jordan).

Imagine living through all of this and not being affected by the stress. If you or a family member has served in one of the United States Armed Forces (Army, Marine Corps, Navy, Air Force, and Coast Guard) or as a first responder or volunteer in relief efforts, thank you for your service to our country.

Lifestyle Changes Also Cause Stress

Even "good" events such as job promotions, marriage, vacations, inventions, and all kinds of social and economic trends involve change, and change increases stress. Consider how the following events and advances have changed your family's lifestyle in the last few generations:

- The rapid expansion in *electrical technology* has transformed industry and society. Households and businesses now have electricity to operate appliances, equipment, and machines and provide energy for lighting, heating, and cooking.

- By the 1930s, most of the *mechanical technology* used in today's automobiles was invented. Now, 95 percent of American households own a car, and 85 percent of Americans get to work by car.[9]

- The *Nineteenth Amendment* to the US Constitution guarantees all American women the right to vote. This lengthy and difficult struggle lasted decades.

- During the 1950s, *television* became the primary medium for molding public opinion. In the mid-1960s, color broadcasting surged in the United States. About 98 percent of American households have at least one television.

- *Space exploration* continues to make advances in aeronautics and technology development. Commercial space transportation is also on the horizon.

- Although originally designed for simple voice communications, today's *phones* record, send, and receive messages; take and display photographs and video; play music, games, TV, and movies; and surf the internet. Smartphones integrate all mobile communication and computing needs.

- The mass marketing of *personal computers* began in 1977. By 2012, 80 percent of American households (up from 8 percent in 1982) had computers and internet access.[10]

- New vaccines, antibiotics, and other *medical advances* have provided lifesaving benefits. Penicillin antibiotics were the first manufactured drugs to be effective against bacterial infections.

- *Air travel* continues to increase. The US Department of Transportation reports that US airlines carry almost sixty-nine million passengers each month.

- And the list goes on.

There's no escaping change. It's constant and stressful. Lifestyles and social norms keep changing. It's the time and the intensity of stress that can cause serious damage to our brains. How are you coping with the stress? It's your choice how to deal with it.

Choose Well

We all experience stressful and traumatic times, such as losing a loved one, serious injury or illness, family conflicts, or other significant events. There are no cookie-cutter solutions for managing stress, but the best place to start is to become aware of how it's affecting you physically, emotionally, mentally, and spiritually.

Work on letting go of your stress little by little. It's like those Chinese handcuffs that kids put on their fingers. The harder they pull to get out of them, the tighter they get. The longer you hold on to stress, the more the symptoms become part of you.

Give Your Brain a Break!

Every now and then rest your brain. Relaxing can sharpen memory and improve creativity, productivity, and reaction time. These quick tips can decrease your stress and improve your brain function and are more therapeutic than you may think. There are more self-help tools throughout this book as well as hundreds of stress management resources available in bookstores and on the internet.

Please take the following suggestions seriously. At the least, commit to trying some of them and mark this page for frequent review.

- *Say "no."* Something's got to give. Trying to do everything for everybody all the time is a dangerous lifestyle that won't end well. Know your limits, and make sure the people around you are clear on them too. Don't attempt more than you can handle. It's okay to say no; it leaves more time and energy for the yeses. And you don't need to explain yourself or keep apologizing. It may even help those around you develop some independence and skills.

- *Take a catnap.* Ten-minute naps can improve alertness for up to three hours. Anything longer may interfere with nighttime sleep and make you feel groggy.
- *Get lost.* Take short mental breaks and let your mind wander. Get lost in your thoughts and daydream about things you want to see or do.
- *Cheer up your brain.* Our brains are interconnected with our emotions and facial expressions. When people are stressed, it shows in their faces. Laughing and smiling relieve some of that tension and may even improve some situations.
- *Stop the daily grind.* Stress can settle in your jaws. Teeth gritting and grinding cause mental exhaustion, facial pain, damaged teeth, and poor quality sleep. During the day, try putting the tip of your tongue between your teeth to relax jaw muscles when you feel stressed. Stop chewing gum because it keeps your jaw muscles used to clenching. At night, consider a mouth/bite guard (custom-made are best), avoid caffeine and alcohol, and relax your jaw muscles by holding a warm washcloth against your cheek in front of your earlobe.
- *Stand tall.* When people are stressed, they can neglect their posture, as if they're carrying the weight of the world on their shoulders. Over time, certain muscles tighten or shorten while others lengthen and become weak. Poor posture can result in long-term neck, shoulder, and back pain. Slumping also reduces blood and oxygen flow to the brain, restricts

breathing, and tenses muscles. Straightening your spine has the opposite effect; it promotes circulation, increases oxygen levels in your blood, and helps lessen muscle tension, all of which relieve stress.

- *Look forward.* Make plans for special activities in the coming months. It's hard to get away from a stressful job, needy kids, credit card bills, and long lists of projects, but looking forward to something fun like a movie marathon, lunch with friends, or a short road trip can give you a calming perspective. Short, spontaneous breaks are great too.

- *Cut down caffeine.* Caffeine affects people differently, partly because genetics influence our response to caffeine. Its effects are long-lasting and can compound stress or the perception of stress. Caffeine is a mild stimulant to the central nervous system so if you take it habitually, your brain learns when the drug is coming and gets ready to react. Half the time drink caffeine, and the other half drink decaf. Coffee or tea could even be mixed half and half. Your brain will stop associating the drink with a caffeine response. Also switch up when and where you drink caffeine so your brain will stop associating caffeine with those times and places. Wean yourself slowly to avoid caffeine-withdrawal headaches. Over a few weeks, gradually increase the proportion of decaf drinks.

- *Do a five-second shake.* Stress can tighten the muscles in your neck, shoulders, and back. While standing or sitting, look up, stretch your arms out to your sides, and shake your hands hard. Combine this with a smile and a few deep breaths.

- *Eat right.* Foods high in carbohydrates stimulate the release of serotonin, a feel-good brain chemical that helps induce calm. But there are good carbs and bad carbs. People trying to feel better may overeat bad (refined) carbs like potato chips, sugary drinks, and pastries. That's why they may gain weight when stressed.

- *Make two lists.* Get a new perspective by looking at the big picture. Make a list of the stressors you might be able to change or avoid. Make another list of the things you can't change. Change what you can from the first list, such as avoiding heated topics or finding time for yourself. Stop stressing over things out of your control, such as changing your supervisor's management style or healing an elderly parent.

- *Find comfort.* There's something comforting about warmth and darkness. Rub the palms of your hands together fast until they feel warm. Then cup them over your closed eyes and breathe slowly. This common trick is so quick and easy that it can be done almost any time any place. Try it now.

- *Walk it out.* Brief, brisk walks can clear your head and relieve stress. Walking also increases blood circulation and gets more oxygen to the brain. Step outside or find a long hallway. It doesn't matter when or where, just move. It lifts your mood and, even better, grab someone to go with you. It'll make their day.

- *Try the child pose.* Muscles tighten over the course of the day, and when you're stressed, the process speeds up. Stretching loosens muscles and encourages deep breathing. The stress-relieving yoga "child pose" position can calm your mind and body. Find a comfortable place to kneel, sit back on your heels, then lean forward and put your forehead on the floor. Lay your arms by your legs with your palms up, then close your eyes. Ease into this position by relaxing your shoulders and neck. You'll feel a gentle stretch in your shoulders and down the length of your spine and arms. Hold this position for at least two to three minutes.

- *Choose a motto.* Biochemicals flush through your body when the stress response turns on, and your brain goes into an alarm state. Decide on a short, positive statement that calms you, such as "I choose peace" or "I can handle this." Close your eyes and repeat your motto three times every time you feel stressed.

- *Take a mini-time-out.* Count to five before you say or do something you might regret. Step away from the stressor for a moment, walk around the room, or put the caller on hold. Use your mini-time-out to take a few deep breaths, stretch, or recite your calming motto.

- *Breathe in deeply then exhale the stress.* Shallow chest breathing can cause your heart to beat faster and your muscles to tense up, making feelings of stress even worse. Deep belly breathing oxygenates the blood, which helps you relax almost instantly. Inhale slowly through your nose, hold the breath for a few seconds, then exhale slowly and repeat.

- *Adjust your lifestyle* to include more leisure time and healthy relationships. *Build your support system* of family, friends, neighbors, church members, and coworkers. Discuss your concerns with a trusted person. Talking relieves strain, puts things in perspective, and may lead to a plan of action.

- *Practice relaxation techniques* such as progressive muscle relaxation, guided visual imagery, relaxed breathing, meditation, and prayer.

- *Practice positive thinking* such as, "Life is difficult, but not hopeless," "I'll start looking for options," or "Bad choices hurt, so I'll make better choices."

- *Challenge inaccurate thinking* such as, "This situation will never get better," "This is all my fault," "I'll only be happy when . . . ," "No one cares," "I must be perfect," "There's no way out," or "The future is hopeless."

- *Try to avoid* denial, isolation or withdrawal, blaming yourself or others, anger, rationalization, or becoming controlling or passive-aggressive.

- *Focus on healthy behaviors* such as laughter, hope, forgiveness, patience, and kindness.

- *Be realistic.* Set realistic expectations. Prioritize and do the more important things.

- *Avoid self-medication.* Alcohol and over-the-counter drugs can add to your problems.

- Get plenty of *sleep, exercise,* and *good nutrition.*
- *Ask for help.* There are many books and online resources available. Live, individualized counseling and medical assistance may be more helpful to some.

Control Your Stress Before It Controls You

The time to relax is when you don't have time for it.

> Sydney J. Harris, journalist

We live as though there aren't enough hours in the day, but if we do each thing calmly and carefully we will get it done quicker and with much less stress.

> Viggo Mortensen, actor

Much of the stress that people feel doesn't come from having too much to do. It comes from not finishing what they've started.

> David Allen, author

In times of great stress or adversity, it's always best to keep busy, to plow your anger and your energy into something positive.

> Lee Iacocca, businessman

Hack away at the inessentials.

> Bruce Lee,
> martial arts master

Doing something that is productive is a great way to alleviate emotional stress. Get your mind doing something that is productive.

Ziggy Marley, musician

If you ask what is the single most important key to longevity, I would have to say it is avoiding worry, stress, and tension.

George Burns, comedian

Brain Boosters

Historical Ages

BC—Before Christ

(BCE—Before Common Era)

AD—Anno Domini (in the year of the Lord); After Death of Christ

(CE—Common Era)

Circa—approximately or about (c., ca., circ., cca.)

Ancient history (3600 BC–AD 500)

Postclassical Era (500–1500)

Modern history (1500–present)

Is the following sequence of time correct? True or false? The dates may be approximations.

Ends c. 6000 BC–2000 BC	Stone Age
c. 3000 BC–1500 BC	Bronze Age

c. 1200 BC–AD 300	Iron Age
c. 500–1500	Dark Ages and Middle Ages
c. 1300–1600	Renaissance and Reformation
c. 1600–1700	Age of Enlightenment
1776	Declaration of Independence (USA)
1861–65	Civil War
1914–18	World War I
1939–45	World War II
1948	Israel became a nation again
1954–68	Civil rights movement
1980	Internet global system of computer networks
1991	World wide web available to the public
2001	World Trade Center destroyed (USA)
1975, 1982, 1991, 2008	Recent global recessions

True (correct) _____   **False (incorrect)** _____

Historical Personalities

These historical figures are from a range of cultures and countries. Are there any mistakes in the following information?

True False

1. Alexander the Great was the king of Macedonia and conqueror of Greece and Persia by 325 BC. He was taught by Aristotle, who was taught by Plato, who was taught by Socrates.   ____ ____

2. Cleopatra was the queen of Egypt in 51 BC.   ____ ____

3. Julius Caesar was betrayed by Brutus in 44 BC.   ____ ____

	True	False

4. The Allies fought together to defeat the Germans and other Axis countries (Japan, Italy) in World War II (1939–45).

5. Benedict Arnold was a traitor in the American Revolution in 1780.

6. Napoleon Bonaparte was the French emperor defeated in the Battle of Waterloo in 1815.

7. John Wilkes Booth assassinated President Abraham Lincoln in 1865.

8. Custer was defeated by Sitting Bull in the Battle of Little Bighorn in 1876.

9. Adolf Hitler was the leader of Germany during World War II.

10. Winston Churchill was the prime minister of Britain during World War II (1939–45) and again from 1951–55.

11. $E=MC^2$ is the correlation between mass and energy (E is units of energy, M is units of mass, C^2 is the speed of light squared or multiplied by itself).

12. Thomas Edison, 1847–1931, patented over one thousand inventions.

Psychology and Memory Improvement

Psychology is the study of how the human mind functions, including the attitude, behavior, thinking, and reasoning of who we are. Naturally, it includes how to improve memory.

Good memory is dependent on attention, storage, and retrieval. If any one of these systems is not working properly, you are likely to have memory difficulties.

Are the following statements correct (true) or incorrect (false)?

	True	False

1. Founders of behaviorism included Pavlov and Skinner.

2. Founders of cognitive theory included Piaget and Binet.

3. Founders of functionalism included Lanes and Dewey.

4. Founders of gestalt theory included Perls and Goldstein.

5. Founders of humanistic theory included Rodgers and Rank.

6. Founders of psychoanalysis included Freud and Jung.

7. The Greeks in 500 BC said memory could be improved by visualization and association.

8. Sherrington in 1897 said there are connections between nerve cells. Eccles in 1965 said the synapses could be made "bigger and better" through mental exercises. In 1974 Phelps invented the PET scan and implied that we could someday see the synapses. Dragonski in 2004 did experiments with MRI, showing increased brain volume in humans through mental exercise. Today, we strongly suspect that through exercises described in this book neurogenesis and neuroplasticity are possible.

9. Binet in 1905 did the first IQ test. IQ revolves around memory, vocabulary, and reasoning.

10. Memory is involved in vocabulary, concepts (knowledge), and visualization.

5

Anxiety and Your Brain

IT'S A FACT: Approximately forty million adults in America are being medicated for anxiety.[1] If you don't manage it, it will manage you.

Anxiety is an internal feeling (pointing inward) of apprehension or fear.

Is Your Brain Being "Wired" for Anxiety?

Anxiety is not only hard to live with but also robs your happiness and impacts your mental abilities. Chronic anxiety can affect areas of the brain that influence long-term and short-term memory. An imbalance of hormones can also impact the brain's chemistry and the production and balance of neurotransmitters. Basically, the more chronic the anxiety, the more neural pathways can become "wired" for anxiety. But the changes to the brain are treatable with medical management and by making some changes to your daily life.

For example, if you don't want your concentration to become a problem, you need to get anxiety under control. It takes a lot of mental energy to focus on tasks and situations throughout the day. Depending on the severity of your anxiety, this can be difficult and may actually reduce your productivity and quality of life.

Anxiety also increases your chances of mental decline as you age. With the increasing interest in the causes and progression of mental decline, studies are underway to help us get a better understanding of how chronic anxiety damages cognition and brain structure over a period of time. More specifically, how it relates to cognitive delay, dementia, and Alzheimer's disease. There is enough concern that clinicians are encouraged to routinely screen for anxiety in people who have memory problems.

Are You Struggling with Anxiety Overload?

Do you know someone who is trying to cope with persistent anxiety? Is it you?

Too many people are dealing with the emotional and physical pain of anxiety. It affects relationships, occupational success, leisure and social activities, and other important areas of their lives.

About one-third of the population will have an anxiety disorder sometime during their lifetime. It's the most common of all psychiatric disorders, but it's good to know that people can benefit from self-help practices and short- or long-term professional care. I want everyone to recover, so they can live normally and think clearly.

I remember working with Joan at the Clinic. She was always tired, tense, and had trouble concentrating at work. She was irritable and wasn't sleeping well. Joan believed everything she was thinking. Her negative self-talk had become a bad habit of thinking the worst would always happen. The anxiety was coming from vague apprehension and fears about every aspect of her life. I told her, "I can help relieve your symptoms with medicine, but they need to work in conjunction with you making changes in your routines and thinking patterns. These working together will make a lasting difference." Joan's recovery was a lengthy but successful process. Months of cognitive behavioral treatment were supported by the self-help tools she still practices today. She has her personality back. She has her peace and vitality back. She has her mental health back.

Symptoms Can Be the Tip of the Iceberg

Everyone experiences bouts with anxiety now and then. We feel it when there are problems at work or when making important decisions. It's a normal reaction and can actually be beneficial in some situations.

For some people, though, it becomes excessive. They dwell on money problems, past hurts, or workplace issues. These are the most common worries that knock people off balance. Their anxiety shows in spite of efforts to keep it under wraps. I can hear the tension in their voices even when they claim they are calm. They have difficulty controlling the symptoms. To make things worse, their anxiety affects the people around them.

Anxiety can be a serious mental illness when the symptoms become constant and overwhelming. But with appropriate treatment, many people can manage those feelings and get back to a fulfilling life. Anxiety disorders are highly treatable, but only about one-third of those suffering receive professional care.

Medical statistics show that people with an anxiety disorder are three to five times more likely to go to the doctor for other reasons. It's not uncommon for someone with severe anxiety to also suffer from depression, and vice versa. Nearly one-half of those diagnosed with depression are also diagnosed with an anxiety disorder.[2]

Have you personally experienced the symptoms of prolonged anxiety? The constant uneasiness, nervousness, dread, worry, and apprehension are exhausting. It's a feeling that something must be done but not knowing what. An anxious person might be irritable, fidgety, overdependent, or hyperalert. He or she may talk too much or have difficulty falling asleep, frequent headaches and other aches and pains, a quivering voice, butterflies in the stomach, and other uncomfortable symptoms.

An anxiety disorder is medically determined by having at least three or more of the following symptoms (with at least some symptoms *present for more days than not for the past six months*). Don't downplay any of these symptoms. They all interfere with the ability to think clearly.

- irritability
- difficulty falling or staying asleep, or restless, unsatisfying sleep

- restlessness or feeling keyed up or on edge
- easily fatigued
- difficulty concentrating or mind going blank
- muscle tension

The levels of anxiety are a little complicated, but they are important to know because each level of anxiety provokes the next, and each disrupts healthy brain functioning. To some degree, all three levels need to be addressed to resolve the disorder.

Level #1 is from childhood stress issues, abuse, or abandonment.

Level #2 is from current situations that are upsetting. Level #1 can intensify #2.

Level #3 is like anxiety over anxiety. Levels #1 and #2 can be suppressed and redirected to this level. Displaced anxiety can be seen in obsessive-compulsive disorder and phobias.

Worry, Fear, and Stress Are Much Like Anxiety

All four of these feelings involve preoccupation with something that eventually causes mental damage. But they differ in the causes and ways they affect a person.

Anxiety points more toward an unknown cause.

Fear points more toward a known cause.

Worry points more inward.

Stress points more outward.

But all of these conditions involve

- tension and apprehension over a (known or unknown) danger
- feelings of foreboding, apprehension, or uneasiness
- unpleasant anticipatory dread or distress
- feelings that something must be done but not knowing what
- a symptom of another emotional disorder
- often physical symptoms

The Causes Are Complex

Please find comfort in knowing that anxiety disorders are not caused by a character flaw or personal choice, nor are they your or somebody else's fault. They are caused by a combination of risk factors involving brain chemistry, life events or environmental stress, personality, and genetic factors. Certain anxiety disorders are due to changes in the brain circuits that regulate fear and memories linked with emotions. Childhood trauma works like this.

Studies show that these disorders can partly be inherited from one or both parents, like the genetic risks for heart disease or cancer. There are also things in life that can "pull the trigger on the genes" such as stress, poor health, or drugs. Environmental influences such as trauma or a significant event may also trigger an anxiety disorder in people who have an inherited susceptibility to developing the disorder.

More generally, anxiety can be learned by example (identifying with an anxious parent), come from chronic conflicts, or even come from being anxious about being anxious. In any case, it's important to recognize unhealthy anxiety as early as possible and get help to stop the pain and damage.

The Different Types of Anxiety Disorders Have Some Symptoms in Common

Collectively the various types of anxiety disorders are among the most common mental health issues. In each type, some of the same symptoms are present, but the effects, impulses, and treatments may vary. The biochemical and anatomical abnormal reactions also vary. In some, the neuroendocrine dysfunction slows thinking, increases cortisol, and causes chronic fatigue.

Targeted medications may temporarily help with some of the symptoms, but this isn't the only or the most complete treatment option. There are techniques to train the brain and manage life in a more balanced, calm way. Studies show that regular mental and physical exercise can significantly reduce symptoms. And of course, behavioral therapy can help control anxiety levels in the long term.

Each type of anxiety disorder has some distinct symptoms.

Generalized Anxiety Disorder

The general symptoms are excessive, unrealistic worry and tension, even if there's little or nothing to provoke the anxiety. Other symptoms are fatigue, restlessness, decreased concentration, irritability, muscle tension, and sleep disturbance.

The person finds it difficult to control the constant sense of worry. It's often present with depression and other types of anxiety.

Social Anxiety Disorder

We all have a little social anxiety but not to the point where it becomes a chronic social disorder. "What will they think about me?" "What if I'm called on to speak?" "Will I embarrass myself?" The fears are not about storms, heights, illness, injury, or death but about social situations, and they tend to lead to social withdrawal.

Most common in females, it involves an exaggerated negative emotion without any cognitive control. It may start gradually in childhood or adolescence. The person has an excessive, persistent, and unreasonable fear of social or performance situations. There is blushing, sweating, increased heart rate, and sometimes nausea and diarrhea. Abnormal brain functioning and cognitive distortions include exaggerated humiliation, excessive self-focus, and impaired concentration.

It usually centers on a fear of being judged by others or behaving in a way that might cause embarrassment. This anxiety may be fueled by a fear of public speaking, starting conversations, attending parties, dating, or being in small groups.

Obsessive-Compulsive Disorder

This often centers on a recurrent theme and a specific unreasonable thought, such as fear of germs or dirt. To ease the thought, the person may compulsively wash their hands until they're sore. The unwanted urges and actions keep coming back despite efforts to ignore them. This increases the distress, which leads to more ritualistic behaviors. It's a vicious cycle.

On a less intense level, if you have recurring thoughts that become obsessive, put up a fight against them. Work to replace those thoughts with healthy actions. Try the Label Principle. It's simple and works with any worry, obsession, habit, or thought pattern you want to change.

Step 1: *Label* the thought. When an unwanted thought invades your mind, label it for what it is—an obsession or worry that is a useless recurrent thought. Say to yourself, "Now you are obsessing."

Step 2: *Limit* the thought. Say silently to yourself, "Now stop obsessing."

Step 3: *Redirect* the thought with either mental exercises or physical exercise. Change your obsessions to healthy actions like a project, walking the dog, or reading an entertaining book.

Step 4: *Release* any other worries by talking about them with someone.

Post-Traumatic Stress Disorder

Military veterans can suffer post-traumatic stress disorder (PTSD) after combat or acts of terrorism. Many other traumatic experiences in which life is threatened result in this long-term, intense fear. Examples include a physical or sexual assault, being threatened with a weapon, witnessing a death or injury to another, suffering from a natural disaster, being in a fire or serious accident, or the sudden death of a close person.

Symptoms can include recollections and dreams of the event, avoiding anything associated with the event, less interest in life, feelings of detachment, difficulty with sleeping and concentrating, anger, and hypervigilance.

I've been particularly interested in helping those with post-traumatic stress disorder. One reason relates to my deep respect for my dad and his soldier friends. Dad was in World War II. He was tough—a man of integrity, bravery, and kindness. Raymond was Dad's friend. He too was tough and brave. But Raymond suffered from shell shock and never talked about his malady. He hurt, no doubt, but kept the pain inside and suffered even more because of it. Today thousands have PTSD but help is available.

Phobic Disorder

Phobias are excessive, persistent fears and anxiety over a specific object or situation, such as heights, flying, or a certain type of animal. The level of fear is usually inappropriate to the situation and may cause the person to avoid even everyday situations.

Adjustment Disorder

Also known as situational depression, this is an excessive reaction to a stressful life event like a flood, fire, marriage, divorce, new baby, new school, or new job. Stressors may also be recurrent or continuous events like marital problems, severe business issues, a child witnessing parents' constant fighting, chemotherapy or other periodic unpleasant medical treatments, financial difficulties, or living in a dangerous area.

Anxiety attacks are moments of extreme anxiety, rapid heartbeat, trembling, sweating or chills, shortness of breath, dizziness, fear of dying, or "going crazy." The feelings of terror strike suddenly and repeatedly with no warning. Other symptoms include chest pain, irregular heartbeat, and a feeling of choking. It can feel like a heart attack.

The duration is limited by a period of time, and the reason is identifiable. There is usually a significant problem in social, occupational, or academic functioning. These factors increase the risk of substance abuse and suicide. Treatment is available and necessary.

Panic Disorder

"All of a sudden, I was overcome with fear. My heart pounded and it was hard to breathe. I broke out in a sweat and shook. I thought I was going to die," recounted a patient. Panic attacks are brought on by thoughts or events of intense fear that trigger severe physical reactions when there is no real danger.

Symptoms include debilitating anxiety, strange chest sensations, shortness of breath, dizziness, tingling, trembling, and rapid heartbeat and can result in hyperventilation, agitation, or withdrawal.

Panic disorders often begin in the late teens, but many people have just one or two attacks in their lifetimes, and the problems go away. Typical examples are an irrational fear of driving, flying in airplanes, or riding in crowded elevators, and these fears can become phobias.

Anxiety Due to a General Medical Condition

The symptoms for this type of anxiety can include those of the other disorders and are directly linked to the person's medical condition. There must be a close association between the medical condition and anxiety in order for this diagnosis to be correct. That is, the anxiety symptoms must occur close in time to the onset or worsening of the medical condition.

Advances Are Being Made toward Managing Anxiety

In the future, more effective treatments will be developed to increase the success and duration of relief from anxiety. Continuing progress has been made in areas of anxiety research and correlations.

1961	systematic desensitization for anxiety
1967	life changes and effects on anxiety
1975	PET scans and evidence of anxiety
1976	practicing choice to help anxiety
1986	nerve cell effects of anxiety
1987	Prozac to help anxiety
1989	MMPI-2 (Minnesota Multiphasic Personality Inventory) published, the most widely used psychometric test for measuring adult psychopathology of all types
1990	genetic causes of and associations with anxiety

1991	learned optimism and effect on anxiety
2000s	biological psychology shows synaptic and neuron changes from anxiety
2013	diagnosis of anxiety (overlapping symptoms and comorbidities)

Work continues for more effective treatments including medications and hybrid treatment options.

The Rest Is Up to You

Now that you know more about anxiety, you have a far greater chance of managing and recovering from the disruptive symptoms. It's best to recognize them in the early stages before the harmful thought patterns become chronic. But it's never too late to fight to restore your mental health.

Anxiety disorders can't always be prevented, but there are things that can be done to control and ease the symptoms. You may be able to reduce the emotional bondage and find the peace you long for. Your response to suffering is sometimes even more important than knowing the reasons for it. Please study the following Choose Well section for helpful tips.

Choices We Can Make

Anxiety is such an ostensibly simple term,
    or is it?
Anxiety is such a ubiquitous, unconquerable
    villain,
    or is it?

Is anxiety innocuous,
   or is it rather insidious?
Are its henchmen ready to attack?
Do an array of menacing mischiefs wait at the
   door?
Is anxiety complex?

Many nuances, many dangers, many faces—all
   apply.
Idiosyncratic, indomitable, imperious—all
   describe.
But are the complexities insurmountable?

Legions of angels are at our beck and call.
Choices we can make.
Options we have been given.
Anxiety can abate.

                      Dr. Frank Minirth

Choose Well

If anxiety is threatening your brain health, the following self-help tools can help you manage it in the moment and build a long-term plan. *Though simple, the advice is powerful and can help get anxiety under control.* Please read through this list every week for the next few months, and use these tips. In time, they will bring you relief and healing.

1. *Stop consuming caffeine*, or drastically reduce products that contain caffeine, such as coffee, tea, cola, energy drinks, and chocolate.
2. *Consult a doctor* or pharmacist before taking any over-the-counter medicines or herbal remedies.

Many contain chemicals that can increase anxiety symptoms.

3. *Consider the odds*. About 95 percent of worries never come true, and most of life's catastrophes we never see coming. Worry is useless.

4. *Live one day at a time*. Obsessive worriers live in the future; depressive worriers live in the past. The future is not here; the past is gone. Live in the present.

5. *Get the facts*. Worries often fade with facts. Perhaps the big picture has been missed. Facts will help.

6. *Share with a friend*. A very true, old adage says, "A burden shared is only half a burden." Build a few close friendships, and share often. Talk through your problems to get a fresh perspective. A study on communication determined that the average busy person spends 80 percent of their day communicating. The breakdown was 45 percent listening, 30 percent talking, 16 percent writing, and 9 percent reading.[3]

7. *Use the time-limit technique*. Limit "worry time" to a specific fifteen-minute period every morning and another fifteen-minute period in the evening. Refuse to worry nonstop because it wastes your time and saps your energy.

8. *Consider the probability*. If the worry just won't go away, then take action. Prepare for the worst, and then improve on it (though often, the worst will not happen).

9. *Make a plan of action*. When troubles come, plan options, list good and bad options, then list crazy

options. Then choose a few options you can implement now.

10. *Relax.* When you feel tense, drop your shoulders and breathe deeply. Then tense your hands, feet, and facial muscles, hold it, then release.

11. *Use a repetitive phrase* (or visualize a favorite retreat) to help you unwind. Decide on a phrase like "calm down." When feeling anxious, say it over and over, and soon the phrase will trigger the desired action. Time and conditioning are required to make this method dependable.

12. *Listen to soothing music.* Did you ever wonder why stores provide easy listening music? It helps people slow down, so they can relax and stay longer in the present situation.

13. *Spend more time in a positive environment* with supportive people. Share laughter, forgiveness, and patience.

14. *Regular aerobic exercise* reduces the level of stress-related hormones in the body. Start a graduated exercise routine, and stick with it.

15. *Eat a healthier diet* and avoid eating late at night. Skipping meals lowers your metabolic rate and energy level.

16. Emotions are often "light sensitive." *Bring more light* into your home and office by opening your curtains and turning on another light. Find a hue that calms you—certain bulbs or light sources have pinkish, yellowish, or bluish tints.

17. *Get adequate sleep*. Most people need an average of seven and one-half hours of sleep per night.

18. *Guard your diet*. Excessive sugar, alcohol, coffee, tea, and soft drinks can rob your system of the nutrients and energy it needs to manage anxiety.

19. *Reduce anxiety through cognitive choices*. Choices are powerful in directing your daily life. Anxiety's source is in the mind, and it must be controlled, challenged, and redirected. It may help to rank your worries. Using a scale of 1 to 5, with 1 being a minor hassle and 5 being a crisis, assign a number to your worries. Those in the 1 to 3 range aren't a big deal. Let them go.

20. *Better beliefs are needed*. Inaccurate beliefs can increase anxiety. You can help keep your anxiety under control if you challenge cognitive distortions:

    "I'm not perfect. I'll move toward growth and forgive myself when I fail."

    "This situation is not the end of the world. God has everything under control."

    "I'm focusing too much on the negative. Much has gone well in my life."

    "Just because I think something is true does not mean it is true."

    "The future is not hopeless. Good can come out of bad."

    "Life is difficult but not hopeless. I can fight back."

"Choosing bad thoughts hurts, so I will choose
   healthy thoughts."

"People care to different degrees, often depending
   on their maturity levels."

"Options may be difficult to see, but options do
   exist. I'll start looking."

"Two are better than one."

21. *Control your attitude.* "I am convinced that life is 10
    percent what happens to me, and 90 percent how I
    react to it."[4]

22. *Lighten up.* Be aware of your attitude. Limit your
    negativity, smile and laugh more often, don't stew
    about little things, and look for the good in people
    and situations.

23. When you're feeling overwhelmed by details,
    remember to *focus on the big picture.* It may help
    you prioritize the details that are demanding your
    attention.

24. *Appreciate the good things* in your life. It's difficult to
    experience the feelings of anxiety and gratitude at
    the same time.

25. *Seek help* if you regularly feel anxious with no appar-
    ent cause. The encouragement and counsel from a
    professional can help put you in touch with the core
    issues and develop a plan to deal with them.

26. *Get a medical evaluation* and follow-up care.

27. *Get counseling* for insights, behavior (stress reduc-
    tion), and cognition support.

28. The brain records personal fears, anxieties, and trials. Knowing *why you hurt* might direct you toward the solutions.

29. *Get spiritual support.* People who are ill often ask spiritual questions in seeking comfort, meaning, and hope. They can draw on their spiritual beliefs and experience as a source of strength. Meditation and prayer can help the mind relax and focus.

30. And finally, *make a plan and take action.* "Pray to God but row to shore" (Russian proverb).

Brain Boosters

Music

do, re, mi, fa, so, la, ti, do

There are strong correlations between music and academic achievement. Other musical values include artistic, aesthetic, practical, social, entertainment, therapeutic, self-affirmation, and economic benefits.

Is the following information about music events and/or musicians correct? Answer true or false concerning the time sequence and all the facts. (Dates may be approximations.)

		True	False
c. 1000 BC	Medieval period: mostly Christian music survived	___	___
c. AD 1500	Renaissance: humanistic music	___	___

		True	False
c. 1700	Baroque with intensity: Bach's *Mass in B Minor*, Handel's *Messiah*, and Vivaldi's *Four Seasons* Opera is an example.		
c. 1800	Classical with balance in music: Mozart's *The Marriage of Figaro*, Beethoven's *Symphony No. 9*, and Haydn's symphonies and concertos		
c. 1850	Romantic period with emotional feelings emphasized Beethoven's *Moonlight Sonata* was a bridge to this period. Chopin—the "poet of the piano"		
c. 1860	Nationalism with a patriotic flavor: "Dixie" and "Battle Hymn of the Republic"		
c. 1900	Neoclassical period (jazz, folk songs): Copland's *Appalachian Spring* and Stravinsky's *Firebird*		
c. 1900	Expressionism with harmony distortion for expressive effect: Schoenberg's *Pierrot Lunaire*		
c. 1900	Impressionism with focus on emotions: Debussy's "Clair de Lune" and prelude to the "Afternoon of a Faun"		
c. 1930	Modernism with diverse musical styles; no dominant music genre		
c. 1980	Postmodernism, a continuation of electronic and diverse music: Michael Jackson, King of Pop		

Judgment Exercises

Judgment is the ability to make considered decisions or come to sensible conclusions. It is discernment, common sense, perception, wisdom, sharpness, reasoning, acuity, and astuteness.

> Good judgment comes from experience, and a lot of that comes from bad judgment.
>
> Will Rogers, philosopher

Judgment can decrease with decreased cognition and memory. Work to keep your judgment skills sharp. For example, if you were in a theater and someone yelled, "Fire," what would you do (in order of preference)?

Now, consider a more difficult scenario. If you found a letter on the street with an address on it, what would you do?

6

Science Offers Hope

IT'S A FACT: Genes are responsible for the characteristics we inherit. But the choices we make determine the course of our lives.

Every person over thirty is at risk of mental decline.

Risk Factors: Vary by age, social and psychological development, ethnic/cultural identity

Individual Factors: Behavior, personality, education, genetic and physical makeup, lifestyle choices, medical conditions

Family and Environmental Factors: Circumstances, experiences, peer influences, surroundings, community conditions

Transitioning to Midlife

We tend to pause at each milestone decade to consider our achievements and goals. Those entering their thirties and forties begin reassessing their careers and lifestyles. They realize that they're aging and are aware that they need to make changes while they still have time.

Versions of the dreaded midlife crisis have surfaced. For some, it's an emotional time of identity and self-confidence. "Can I stay successful and satisfied?" "Am I passing my peak performance?" "What can I do to stop a downhill slide?"

Many middle-agers experience challenges, such as:

- dealing with mental stress due to caring for family (raising children, empty nest, aging parents)
- extending self-assessments to career, responsibilities, and family
- looking more to the past than the future
- realigning goals because of a feeling that time is running out
- adjusting from idealism to realism
- worrying about health issues
- testing lifestyle changes for better or worse

But there are cognitive upsides to these years too:

- renewing interest in losing weight and getting in shape
- reconnecting with high school and college friends
- wanting to feel better, look younger, and have healthier habits
- enjoying more time for themselves
- wanting to learn new things and expand their interests

- exploring new types of entertainment and hobbies
- enjoying different settings and destinations for vacations
- restarting things that were dropped twenty years earlier
- hanging out with younger generations for stimulation
- finding new solutions to problems
- and, best of all, realizing the importance of brain fitness

As we grow older, we hope to avoid cognitive decline and dementia. We're counting on medical advances for near-miracle drugs and treatments, but we also need to take personal responsibility. Science is proving that regardless of age, we can keep developing new brain cells and building more connections to boost our mental capabilities. But this is a personal challenge that requires commitment and action.

An estimated 6.8 million Americans currently have dementia and 5.4 million suffer from Alzheimer's disease. Of the 5.4 million, about 5.2 million people are age sixty-five and older (the others have younger-onset Alzheimer's).[1] These conditions are robbing people of their memory and dignity and profoundly affecting the lives of their loved ones.

These numbers are rapidly escalating because the baby boomer generation is reaching their vulnerable senior years. This includes people born after World War II between 1946 and 1964. These people are at the greatest risk of Alzheimer's.[2]

If this trend continues, based on population projections by the US Census Bureau, the number of Alzheimer's patients over sixty-five may nearly triple by 2050. Barring the development of medical breakthroughs to prevent or cure the disease, there may be thirteen to sixteen million Americans with dementia.[3]

Global Focus on Dementia Research

A worldwide effort is underway to find new treatments to prevent, slow down, and end Alzheimer's. As part of international summits to discuss economic concerns, energy, health, food supplies, and other areas of common interest, the world's leading nations are developing an international action plan for dementia research. In this unprecedented collaboration, they are sharing information and data. The research includes the anatomy, neurology, physiology, biochemistry, pharmacology, and psychopharmacology related to types of dementias, Alzheimer's disease, and related aspects of cognition.[4]

On the home front, the US National Alzheimer's Project Act has the ambitious goal of "preventing or effectively treating Alzheimer's" by 2025. Studies are also underway by scientists at the National Institutes of Health, the National Institute of Mental Health, and other federal research agencies. These efforts are being supported by private foundations and industries. The cooperation among these agencies and thousands of scientists and health-care professionals gives us hope that brain disease can be conquered.[5]

The Advancements Are Encouraging

Congress designated 1990–2000 as the Decade of the Brain. George W. Bush signed a Presidential Proclamation to introduce cutting-edge research and encourage public dialogue on the ethical, legal, philosophical, and social implications of emerging information and discoveries.

The years 2000–2010 were a decade of brain imaging as technical advances in neuroscience gained widespread use and public visibility.[6]

- *Identifying and diagnosing people at risk* have been improved through PET scans, neurocognitive testing, genome studies, and specific proteins in blood.
- *Neuroimaging* is a relatively new discipline to diagnose intracranial disease such as tumors, injury, metabolic diseases and lesions, and on a finer scale, Alzheimer's disease.

  Advanced brain imaging devices such as amyloid PET scans can identify Alzheimer's in early stages by finding the presence of beta-amyloid and tau protein deposition in people, even before symptoms.
- Studies are revealing *Alzheimer's susceptibility genes* and the use of biomarkers in people with no symptoms yet. Hopefully the results will lead to more information about mutations and treatment targets. Recent studies suggest it may only be through early intervention (before symptoms appear) that the dementia stage of Alzheimer's can be prevented.[7]
- *New theories* concerning synapses and neuronal circuitry under genetic factors will influence drug development in the future.
- Neuroscientists are mapping the *brain's biochemical circuitry*, which may help produce more effective

drugs for Alzheimer's and Parkinson's disease. Increased neurocircuitry can possibly improve with ECT (electroconvulsive therapy), VNS (vagal nerve stimulation), TMS (transcranial metallic stimulation), and DBS (deep-brain stimulation).

- There is also hope for the development of prescription *medications* (chemical inhibitors or stimulators), nerve growth factor agents, stem cell therapies, gene interference therapy, and metabolism-based therapies.

New Drugs Are in Development

Alzheimer's causes physical changes in the brain, and many drugs in development are targeting these changes. Although some of the drugs tested in the past ten years have failed due to negative side effects, the number of promising clinical trials of new drugs is increasing. Some trials target disease prevention, while others are testing drug effectiveness in treatment of symptoms.

There are promising targets for the next generation of drug therapies for dementias, including immunotherapies, gamma globulin, inhibitors and statins for preventing amyloid plaque, antibodies, inhibitors with insulin-sensitizing effects, gene therapy, and others. Researchers believe successful treatment will eventually involve a "cocktail" of medications aimed at several targets, similar to treatments for cancers and AIDS.[8]

To date, five drugs have been approved by the US Food and Drug Administration (FDA) to treat the symptoms of

Alzheimer's disease. They may also help in treating early cognitive decline. These drugs temporarily help memory and thinking problems in about half of the people who take them. They don't treat the underlying causes of Alzheimer's but may slow the progression of dementia.

- Aricept (donepezil)—used in all stages of dementia (1996)
- Exelon (rivastigmine)—all stages (2000)
- Razadyne (galantamine)—mild to moderate cases (2001)
- Namenda (memantine)—moderate to severe cases (2003)
- Namzaric (donepezil and memantine)—moderate to severe cases (2014)[9]

Other drugs and treatments in use are Axona, Vayacog, the Exelon Transdermal Patch, and Cerefolin NAC, an amino acid that has antioxidant effects.

Keep in mind that while medications can be helpful, they can also have a dark, unexpected side. At times, some medications used for other medical issues can actually decrease cognition and memory, for example:

- benzodiazepines (Xanax, Valium, Ativan, Klonopin)
- anticholinergics (tricyclic antidepressants, antipsychotics, skeletal muscle relaxants, anti-Parkinson's drugs, antiemetics [antinausea])
- sedating medications

New Brain Cells and Connections Can Be Developed at All Ages

Neuroplasticity (changing and increasing brain cell connections) and neurogenesis (birth and growth of brain cells) hold great promise for increasing and extending cognition—thinking, understanding, learning, and remembering—into old age.

Neuroplasticity

Neuroplasticity is the formation of new connections between nerve cells. During the past few decades, neuroscientists have built the case that the mature brain is more plastic—changing and malleable—than was thought. The number of these synapses can be increased with mental exercise and learning. These connections can rapidly change even within minutes of stimulation. This is widely touted today because it's important for mental ability in all ages. It helps people communicate better, be more productive at work, and manage life skills.

The brain's neurons (nerve cells) have dendrites that branch out to connect with other neurons. The more branching there is, the more communication there is between cells. The more active the brain is, the smarter one can become. There is more dendritic branching when a person is challenged to think, make comparisons, make inferences, and try new things. This is why a stimulating environment for children through adolescence (and beyond) is so important. There is less dendritic branching if a person passively watches TV all day or repeats tasks without thinking or analyzing.

It is well documented that Albert Einstein had slow verbal development in childhood.[10] He may have had fewer of these nerve cells than average but many more connections. He built and strengthened them through his dedication to hard mental work.

Education is one of the best ways to increase the potential for *memory storage*. For example, studies show that people with college educations have more dendritic branching in their brain cells than those with a high school education. On the other hand, these dendritic fields can be decreased by age, stress, illness, and injury. Decreasing chronic stress and getting adequate sleep are helpful interventions.[11]

Neurogenesis

Neurogenesis is a term that means the brain is capable of creating new cells. This works especially fast in young people. The exciting news is that neurogenesis can work for older people too. Mental exercise is the key. Neurogenesis can also be stimulated by physical exercise that increases oxygen to the brain and provides stress reduction. Some antioxidants, such as omega-3 fatty acids and vitamins C, E, D, B_6, B_9, and B_{12}, may also help.

Who We Are Revolves around Several Factors

Our intelligence and memory depend on our genome (DNA makeup), epigenetic factors, and choices. Each of these can be altered to a degree, but the one that can be altered the most is choice.[12]

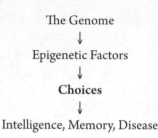

The Genome
↓
Epigenetic Factors
↓
Choices
↓
Intelligence, Memory, Disease

"What is bred in the bone will never come out of the flesh." This proverb means we inherit certain characteristics from our ancestors, and those characteristics can be inherited by our descendants by the laws of genetics. Genetics is the science of how traits are passed from generation to generation. We cannot change how genes transfer from one generation to another (at least at this point in scientific development). The genome is the entire set of genetic instructions in the nucleus of each cell. It governs the makeup and development of each person. Each cell has two sets of genes—one from each parent.

Many experts think that along with aging, genes and lifestyle contribute to the majority of Alzheimer's and dementia cases. Our heredity and chronological age factors can't be changed, but lifestyles can.

To some degree, the aging process is a lifelong accumulation of mutations in our genes. The changes start at the basic cellular level. Examples of the aging process include:

- decrease in cerebral blood flow and metabolism
- slower reflexes and reaction times
- changes in balance

- changes in sleep patterns
- decline in number of nerve cells
- slower nerve conduction
- plaques, tangles, and atrophy of the brain
- accumulation of free radicals
- dulling of tactile sensation
- decline in function of cranial nerves affecting taste and smell
- slower mental processing speed
- reduction in lean body mass, total body fat increases
- decrease in intracellular fluid (the water inside cells makes up about 42 percent of the total body weight)[13]

The health of the nervous system is affected by all other body systems. It's encouraging to know that there are numerous areas of genetic research underway, including classical genetics, molecular genetics, population genetics, and quantitative genetics. More specifically, genomics, comparative genomics, model organisms, molecular biology, genome-wide association studies, bioinformatics, and pharmacogenetics are being researched.

The completion of the sequencing of the human genome was accomplished in 2001. In 2005 the FDA approved a "gene chip" for genotyping variations in the genes that show how effective certain medications are in an individual person according to DNA extracted from their blood. It can identify an enzyme produced by a gene that changes the body's ability to break down (metabolize) certain drugs, such as antidepressants, antipsychotics, beta-blockers, and some chemotherapy drugs.[14] Genotyping is not yet widely available for all medications but can aid in many personalized treatments.

Greater understanding of the genome will hopefully lead to new treatments, drugs, and cures for diseases such as cancer and Alzheimer's. Genetic involvement in mental disorders will also be a focus for future drug development. The genetic factor in early-onset Alzheimer's dementia has been well established, but the late-onset is less clear due to the effects of aging.

Epigenetics are the processes that go on outside the genes. These changes have a major influence on our development because they can switch genes on or off. Natural positive (God-intended) epigenetic changes occur in utero (due to hormone exposure, etc.) to determine which cells develop into blood cells versus bone cells, skin cells, liver cells, brain cells, and so on. Epigenetic changes can also have damaging, mutating effects on cells resulting in diseases like cancer. Epigenetic factors can pull the trigger for good or bad. They can be influenced by age, the environment, lifestyle, and disease. New research is uncovering the role of epigenetics in a variety of disorders and diseases.

Our choices are also powerful factors in who we become. Who we are is determined by our genome, epigenetic influences, as well as our choices. In memory and in the decay of memory, choice is often the trump card!

As a psychiatrist, I sometimes cringe when a patient blames their depression or alcoholism solely on "bad genes." Our genetic makeup does affect personal intellectual and emotional potentials, but our degree of wisdom and happiness is not predetermined genetically. There is a difference.

Genes can predispose an individual to getting drunk easier than others, but they don't make a person take a drink in the first place. Genes can also predispose a person toward a clinical depression under stress because of a depletion of norepinephrine in the brain. But our genes don't make us hold grudges, withdraw from supportive relationships, and neglect our health.

These are bad choices that exacerbate or even cause some mental and emotional problems. Natural consequences occur when we make irresponsible choices. But it's easier to blame parents, a spouse, hypoglycemia, or "bad genes" than owning up to poor behavioral choices.

Some people are irresponsible because they choose to be, and others are irresponsible because they lack knowledge. It's my hope that readers of this book will grow in knowledge and put that knowledge into action by choosing to protect their minds.[15]

Choose Well

A Lesson from Scripture

Adam was the father of the human race. He was genetically gifted and ate wonderful food in the Garden of Eden. However, when he made the bad choice of eating the forbidden fruit, it cost him. His bad choice impacted his perfect genome through an epigenetic factor. This made Adam and his descendants physically and emotionally vulnerable.

However, God still blessed him and wants to show his love to all his creation.

The lesson for us is to choose well!

Bad, Good, Better, Best—You Decide

You may be thinking, "I'd like to make better choices and teach my kids how to make good decisions. It seems harder than when I was growing up because now there are more opportunities and options, and the consequences seem more complex. How do I know if my choices are right? Should I follow my head or my heart?" Needless to say, we can't keep flying by the seat of our pants.

Note which of the following tips would be helpful in your circumstances:

- Be clear on your *personal values*. Every choice has a consequence. Make sure your decisions are aligned with your moral and spiritual values.
- *Repeated choices become habits*. Habits make you the person you are. Over time, good choices and bad choices become habits that are hard to break. The neural pathways become automatic. How do you break a bad habit like knuckle cracking or nail-biting? (1) Notice when you're doing it and why. Is it because of stress or boredom? (2) Keep a written tally of each time you do it. You may be surprised how often it is. (3) When you catch yourself, make a conscious effort to resist, relax, and distract. Replace it with a good behavior.

- Having choices in the first place can be a *motivating factor to do the right thing*. You rarely have to make a choice between obvious good and evil, but you can identify when there is a difference between what you *want* to do and what you *should* do.

- The great thing about choices is that you *almost always have more chances* to turn things around if you're going in a wrong direction. The key is to acknowledge it and make a change.

- Improve relationships with your family and build a *good support system*. Ask people you trust for advice in your decision-making processes. You have the power to overhaul bad situations through better choices.

- Don't let poor choices from the past keep you from making better choices now. *Learn from past mistakes* and successes. Poor choices can lower your self-esteem. Today is a blank slate; start fresh.

- Spend more *time on things that matter* instead of wasting so much time on things that don't. Stay aware of what you're doing and if it fits in with your *long-term goals*. A long-term perspective will likely lead you to better decisions.

- Some choices have immediate *consequences*; others may take longer to reward or hurt you. What are some other options or alternatives? Think about the worst and the best things that could happen if you make a certain decision. Are you willing to live with the risks?

- Think about whether your choices *benefit or harm others* who may be involved.
- Make decisions with both your *head and heart.* Be logical but also be aware of your gut instincts.
- God uses *guilt* to influence you to change your mind when you're doing something wrong. If you feel guilty, make changes.
- Making decisions is a *lifelong skill.* Stop making your growing children's decisions. Teach them to practice these tips.

Your daily choices, habits, and willingness to move past failures will direct your days. *Choose well.*

Brain Boosters

There's a trend today for products and quick fixes to halt physical or mental decline, including wonder pills, extreme diets, and fitness crazes. I believe one of the best tools we have for mitigating mental decline is consistent mental exercise. It increases brain cell dendrites and stimulates neuroplasticity and neurogenesis, which not only prevent decline but actually improve brain functioning.

Neurology and Psychiatry

Neuropsychiatry deals with mental disorders attributed to nervous system diseases. It's a subspecialty of psychiatry and is related to neuropsychology and behavioral neurology, which address clinical problems of cognition and behavior caused by brain injury or brain disease.

Are all of the following definitions and concepts correct?[16]

		True	False
1. brain	the portion of the central nervous system located within the skull; the receiver, organizer, and distributor of information for the body; three main parts: the cerebrum, the cerebellum, and the brain stem; weighs approximately three pounds	___	___
2. amino acids	organic acids containing a carboxyl group (COOH) and an amino group (NH_2); the basic units from which proteins are formed	___	___
3. amygdala	the part of the brain's limbic system involving memory and emotionally charged events	___	___
4. autistic	composed of inner thoughts and individual reality; daydreaming and fantasies are common elements	___	___
5. cytochrome P450 enzymes	an enzyme system in the liver that metabolizes most psychiatric and other medical drugs	___	___
6. delirium tremens (d.t.'s)	a severe and sometimes fatal brain disorder that commonly occurs four to five days after cessation of heavy, consistent consumption of alcohol	___	___
7. ego alien	thoughts that are repugnant, recurrent, unwanted, undesired, and not consistent with a person's usual thinking; they occur in obsessive-compulsive anxiety disorder (OCD)	___	___

		True	False
8. generic drug	a bioequivalent drug named by the US Food and Drug Administration (FDA); the brand name is given by the pharmacy company	____	____
9. hallucination	false sensory perceptions that can be auditory, visual, or tactile	____	____
10. hypothalamic/ pituitary/ adrenalaxis (HPA) response	three structures (hypothalamus, pituitary gland, and adrenal gland) that form the basis of the fight-or-flight stress response	____	____

Conceptual Exercises

Conceptual exercises help us develop approaches to how we understand the dynamics of people, science, technology, and the environment. Increasing the ability to work with conceptual problems and relationships can boost brainpower.

Following are analogical examples. Can you identify the relationships?

Contrast:	*hot/cold/sharp/_____*	a. dull b. cutting c. acute d. keen
Similar, contrast:	*ecstatic/happy/sad/_____*	a. melancholic b. glad c. ecstatic d. euphoric

Part, whole:	*hour/day/day/_____*	a. week b. second c. minute d. millisecond
Whole, part:	*USA/Washington, DC/Russia/_____*	a. Moscow b. Bern c. Madrid d. Rome
Type of:	*insect/arthropod/lobster/_____*	a. crustacean b. mollusk c. oyster d. squid
Completion:	*Mexico/City/New York/_____*	a. City b. New York c. New Jersey d. USA
Implicit relationship:	*states/USA/provinces/_____*	a. Canada b. France c. Switzerland d. England
Sound alike:	*Hi/Bye/now/_____*	a. how b. then c. good d. future
Verb tenses:	*come/came/go/_____*	a. went b. got c. bye d. get
Letters reversed:	*CAT/TAC/DO/_____*	a. OD b. DID c. DON'T d. GONE

Example:	*mom/palindrome/bark/_____*	a. onomatopoeia b. semantics c. homonym d. antediluvian
Mathematical equivalents:	>/greater than/</_____	a. less than b. equal c. forget d. abstract
Mathematical opposites:	>/< *greater than/_____*	a. less than b. equal to c. unequal d. ordinal number

PART 2

How to Protect Your Mind

7

Revive Your Purpose

IT'S A FACT: Every time you recall a memory or have a
new thought, a new connection is created in your brain.

As kids, we fantasized about buried treasure in the nearby
woods or money lost in piles of leaves outside store entrances.
We kept our eyes glued to the ground as we walked, scanning for good stuff. There was always potential for finding
something special. We have that same potential in our lives
today. We may have abilities that haven't been developed or
goals that have been forgotten.

I often hear the buzz phrase, "Maximize your potential."
It's fun to think about the potential our kids have. We dream
big dreams for them, but we forget to keep our own visions
in a growing mode.[1]

If I were to ask one hundred people what they ultimately
hope to do or become, I would probably get one hundred different answers. Some may fantasize about being president of

the United States, while others just want to make it through the day. Others' dreams may be to get off alcohol, heal a marriage, or survive cancer. These are all important visions because they are important to us and inspire positive action.

Leroy Eimes, who served the Navigators ministry for over fifty years, once asked a young man what he was going to do with his life now that he had finished school. The young man thought and thought. Finally he said, "I think I'll buy a Buick."

You may wonder if your goals are big or good enough. Maybe you are shortchanging yourself like this young man. Or maybe your goals need to stretch beyond your investment portfolio and the square footage of your home. Your vision will partially pivot around your relationships, and this is healthy. Your family, friends, colleagues, career, and hobbies not only keep you active but also probably support your life purpose.

In an online pop culture survey, some of the most common life goals young people listed are as follows:[2]

- being happy (content, satisfied)
- achieving intellectual growth (educational achievements)
- having financial freedom (wealth)
- having occupational success
- having close relationships
- having peace of mind
- caring for others, being charitable
- fulfilling personal morals (doing the right things, integrity)

- living Christian values
- pursuing passions
- having stability and safety
- being inspiring
- influencing others (leadership)
- being respected
- appreciating nature and beauty
- fulfilling social values (peace, justice, equality)

What Gets You out of Bed Every Day?

What makes you tick? I believe people of all ages want a challenge, big or small, that sets them apart from everyone else. I want every person to convert their dreams into at least some degree of reality.

You made plans for yourself in your twenties, and you will do the same for your thirties and forties. If you're going to make a major change such as moving to another state or redirecting your career, it's likely you'll do it in one of those decades. Your work-life balance and contentment are probably at healthy levels, so it's the perfect time to assess your brain fitness along with your long-range goals. They work together. Your sense of accomplishment, mixed with hope and a can-do confidence, will help clarify your life purpose.

Every invention and masterpiece began with a dream, an intent that shows what's important to us. The brain tries hard to do what we want it to do. Having dreams and a life mission will keep us centered and growing.[3]

Purpose Was My Journey

My mother believed in mental ability and encouraged me throughout my childhood. At age twelve I developed type 1 diabetes mellitus. The prognosis was poor in those days, and I feared I would die young and that, unless I hurried, intellectual acuity would never be mine.

I went through college in three years at the University of Arkansas because funds were low, and I perceived time as short. Just before medical school I met my "Snow White," Mary Alice, and fell in love. She always encouraged me in my pursuits.

In medical school I studied hard not because I enjoyed it, but because I knew I had to. Since then, books have become excellent friends. Medical school was difficult—many days, months, and years of study. I would not leave my study table for hours.

After medical school I entered a psychiatric residency at the University of Arkansas. I had no intention of becoming an atheist as many psychiatrists do. I was offered a job teaching at a conservative seminary, Dallas Theological Seminary. I knew the Bible, but I had no seminary degree. Students complained. So to keep from being a distraction, I started seminary and eventually received a doctorate.

After medical school, psychiatry, and theological training, I essentially belonged to no school. Theologians rejected me because I was a psychiatrist. Psychiatrists rejected me because I was a theologian. Neither understood how I wanted to weave both disciplines together to help people physically, psychologically, and spiritually.

In the years of my thirties, forties, and fifties, book deals came, radio and television appearances came, and my psychiatric practice grew to multiple outpatient clinics and inpatient programs. Oh, there were tough times—disappointments, death of friends, no more television opportunities, no movies materialized, and relying on an old 1989 Oldsmobile. The good times involved my clinical work and a lifetime of delightful conversations and laughter with Mary Alice, my family, and close friends.

I always tried to avoid any kind of negative input. This somewhat antediluvian (old-fashioned) lifestyle brought me happiness. I have lived a dedicated and disciplined lifestyle. I've been blessed with a good memory, so hopefully I can bless others by helping them boost their brainpower and life purpose.

Keep Your Focus on the Big Picture

Without purpose, nations fail and companies go bankrupt. Without purpose, churches wane and people drift. Without purpose, the brain slows. Perhaps you are unsure of or have temporarily lost sight of your life purpose. It's more than acquiring possessions, making money, or traveling the world. There is more than just doing things. It's living purposefully.

Your passions and related activities bring you fulfillment. The things you accomplish with your heart and talents are things that matter. It's your contribution over time that ultimately makes a difference.

Have you considered God's purpose for your life? In 1958 I found purpose, or rather, purpose found me. It was to have a ministry for Christ. I was twelve years old when Christ became my best friend. I never wanted to displease him then or since. I wanted to boost my brain, so I could be effective for him. This commitment always guided my major decisions. When I developed diabetes, I was fearful, but I committed to trust Christ and he blessed me.

Have you ever heard the old adage, "He can't see the forest through the trees"? The "trees" are all the details of a broad issue—in this case, keeping up with the demands of daily life. The "forest" is the big picture of your legacy. Someone who is so consumed with all the details may miss appreciating the results. I've seen this with homemakers who stew for months over a family holiday gathering but miss the joy of the event. I've seen it in workaholics who get burned out and lose their family and friends. They lose their balance and perspective of what really matters in their lives—relationships.

Sometimes it's hard to stay focused because of the barrage of demands on our time. Have you ever been so consumed by busyness that you missed the joy of a milestone? This often happens when people are building their careers, rearing children, or managing the seasons of marriage. When you're feeling overwhelmed by circumstances, stop and think of the big picture. Realize that many of the circumstances that can distract you are just temporary. This can help you prioritize details that consume your time. You'll realize that some projects or activities have nothing to do with supporting your priorities. These need to be phased out. Keep your energy aimed at the things that enhance your core interests. Stay on track.

If you look back and feel guilty that climbing the ladder of success was accomplished at the expense of your marriage, children, church, or health, forgive yourself and reset your focus. The same is true for memory care. If you've ignored regular brain exercise and now fear it's too late, it's not. It's never too late to take care of your mind.

You Can Lead a Purposeful Life

Contrary to common beliefs, statistics show that career retirement does not cause people to die earlier. According to data compiled by the Social Security Administration, a man reaching age 65 today can expect to live, on average, until age 84.3. A woman turning age 65 today can expect to live, on average, until age 86.6. And those are just averages. About one out of every four 65-year-olds today will live past age 90, and one out of ten will live past age 95.[4]

A growing number of Americans are living to age 100. The centenarian population has increased 65.8 percent in the past thirty years.[5] The bottom line is that most people will have over twenty years to enjoy retirement. This is precious time that can be used to make a difference.

Your circumstances and even some goals will change through each life stage, and this is normal. But will your core passions remain the same? Have they been a steady guide through all the years? We all struggle with this.

What do you want from life? What do you excel at? What do you want to accomplish? What do you care about the most? How do you want to be remembered after you die? Anyone over age twenty (which probably includes most readers of this book) needs to consider these questions and think about the following advice:

- *Focus on what consistently feels important* to you. Choose activities that support your goals.
- *Look for the needs of others* and work to make their lives better any way you can.
- Be aware of your feelings but *focus on your behavior.* "You don't do what you do because you feel the way you feel—you feel the way you feel because you do what you do." You may need to read that a few times to fully grasp the concept and apply it to your experiences.[6]
- *Brainstorm about opportunities* and act on the ones that boost your mission.
- *Be realistic* and stay flexible. There are many ways to reach most goals.
- *Keep a balanced lifestyle* physically, mentally, emotionally, and spiritually.
- *Socialize* with others often (attend worship services, participate in activities, and nurture close family and friend relationships).
- *Stay active mentally.*

Write words or phrases below that describe your unique qualities and choices.

1. Special characteristics:

_____

_____

2. Special skills and interests:

_____

_____

3. Key relationships:

_____

_____

4. Top priorities (most valued):

_____

_____

5. Major goals that are aligned with your values:

_____

_____

Now underline the words above that bring you the most joy and fulfillment. Use these words to draft your strategy for living purposefully.

There Will Be Setbacks and Detours

When I wrote *Christian Psychiatry*, I sent the manuscript to six publishers. I received six rejection letters before it was accepted and became a popular reference for many. I'm glad I didn't give up.

We will always face trials and get sidetracked, but that's when we develop character, endurance, and discipline. Think how many times baseball players strike out compared to the number of home runs they hit. You will hit some home runs, bunts, and foul balls, and you'll strike out at other times. That doesn't mean you don't have the potential to hit the ball out of the field.[7]

Most of us won't be remembered in the history books, but it's our right and responsibility to experience the joy of reaching our potential during our time on earth. Don't quit on your vision.

Encouragement

Do you realize that you're the only one of your kind? Nobody else on earth has ever been or will be exactly like you. Your looks, thoughts, movements, humor, and peculiarities are uniquely significant. But if you don't realize what a miracle that is, how are you going to teach your children this amazing truth? How many times do we intend to tell our children they are special but instead say, "*Do* something special." Each of us wants to feel special too, but instead we think, "What have I really *done* with my life?"

Choose Well

In a recent sermon I heard a preacher say, "We don't have any say about the length of our lives, but we do have a say about the legacy of our lives." What do you hope people will say about you when you pass away? Will they know what your priorities and passions were? Are you living purpose-fully now?

In their book *One Month to Live*, authors Kerry and Chris Shook describe how to live a no-regrets life. Following are their principles for a maximum life plan:

Live passionately, living each day as if it were your last.
Love completely, showing others love that transcends and transforms.
Learn humbly, growing through your problems and pain.
And leave boldly, creating a legacy that will impact generations.[8]

The purpose of life is not to be happy. It is to be useful, to be honorable, to be compassionate, to have it make some difference that you have lived and lived well.

Ralph Waldo Emerson, essayist, *Selected Writings*

If you organize your life around your passion, you can turn your passion into your story and then turn your story into something bigger—something that matters.

Blake Mycoskie, founder of Toms Shoes,
Start Something That Matters

Purpose is the reason you journey. Passion is the fire that lights your way.

Unknown

You were put on this earth to achieve your greatest self, to live out your purpose, and to do it courageously.

Steve Maraboli, *Life, the Truth, and Being Free*

The purpose of life is to contribute in some way to making things better.

Robert F. Kennedy, politician

If you don't know where you are going, you'll end up someplace else.

Yogi Berra, baseball manager

Brain Boosters

Explorers' Passions and Purpose

By knowing our forerunners, we are reminded who we are. Consider how these explorers followed their passions. The following facts are in chronological order, but are all the facts true?

Make an extra effort to commit these facts to memory. Amaze your friends and family by dropping this information into conversations.

1. Eric the Red discovered Greenland in 982.
2. Leif Erikson and his Vikings discovered Newfoundland in 1000.
3. Marco Polo traveled to China in 1271.
4. Bartolomeu Dias sailed around the southern tip of Africa in 1488.
5. Christopher Columbus with his small fleet (Niña, Pinta, and Santa Maria) entered the Caribbean Sea in 1492.

6. European explorers traveled to the Spice Islands (Indonesia) in the 1500s.

7. Vasco Nuñez de Balboa crossed Panama to see the Pacific Ocean in 1513.

8. Ponce de Leon searched for "The Fountain of Youth" in Florida but brought back "A Fountain of Death" (tobacco) in 1514.

9. Ferdinand Magellan sailed around the world in 1519–22.

10. Hernán Cortez conquered the Aztecs in Mexico in 1521.

True (correct) _____   **False (incorrect)** _____

8

You Can Preserve Your Mind

IT'S A FACT: The brain accounts for about 20 percent of energy needs, and uses 20 percent of the oxygen and blood circulating in our bodies.[1]

We spend a lot of time thinking about our heart and skin health because they're critical to our well-being and our looks. But how often do we think about caring for our most important organ, the brain?

Turn on the TV, scan magazines, and surf the internet, and you'll see a barrage of advertisements about how a person can look, feel, and stay young. Bald men can grow hair, and there is a miracle cream for every need. People think, "If I just do those exercises or take those pills . . ." The media has gone overboard to keep youthfulness alive. I wish they would give the same attention to promoting brain fitness for people of all ages. But thanks to the widespread use of the internet, many brain health resources are now accessible to almost every household in America. But this leads us to another issue.

What Is Digital Technology Doing to Our Brains?

Wherever we go, we see people of all ages on smartphones, computers, or other electronic devices. Our brains are getting daily doses of the internet, Google, GPS, apps, hundreds of television channels, video games, MP3 players, wireless networks, Bluetooth links, calendar alerts, and calculators. Texts, tweets, updates, reminders, and other distractions are demanding our attention. Will all this screen time change the way we think and learn?

We know that our plugged-in lifestyle will impact our brain function because the complex networks of nerve cells making up parts of the brain actually change in response to certain experiences and stimuli. Some effects are obvious, deliberate, and positive; others are subtle or unknown, unintentional, and negative.

This reminds me of the famous opening paragraph of Charles Dickens's novel *A Tale of Two Cities*: "It was the best of times, it was the worst of times, it was the age of wisdom, it was the age of foolishness, it was the epoch of belief, it was the epoch of incredulity."

This "always on" technology conditions our brains to pay attention to information differently than when we are reading. For better or worse, there are some ways our brains may be rewiring to handle the deluge of stimuli and data, and changing the way we think and behave. Sleep, attention spans, memory development and retention, visual skills, impulse control, and creativity are just a few areas being affected. It may not be a matter of better or worse; it may just be a matter of different.

On the positive side:

- The parts of the brain used for short-term memory and quick decision making are being stimulated.
- Absorbing multiple sources of information and sorting it for future reference is part of what's rewiring our brains and making them more elastic.
- The internet fosters learning and cognitive development and sharpens the ability to scan information. It's about how we use the information that matters.
- Screen media can improve visual-spatial capabilities and the ability to identify details among clutter and increase reaction times.

On the downside, some people say we are "outsourcing our memory."

- The internet, social media, and computer games may be impairing social interactions and relationships, empathy, and personal identity.
- Our brains may be rewiring for distraction, impatience, forgetfulness, inattention, and lack of focus. This may hinder memory retention, complex thought, conversation, patience, and creativity.
- Our brains may be deprived of needed downtime.
- The instant gratification can make it harder to concentrate on and solve complex problems.

The reality is that we don't know how this changing environment will influence our memory and cognitive functioning in the long term. But human brains have been adapting and developing in response to environmental stimuli and experiences for centuries. The best thing we can do is protect and preserve our brains with these scientifically proven techniques.

Reboot Your Self-Help Commitment

There's a lot of evidence that what we do for our brains now can have a big impact on how they function in the years to come. Some of the risks for brain decline can't be controlled, such as a family history of mental illness. But there are many positive factors that we *can* control and that make a significant difference: being married, having at least two close friends, living in or regularly visiting a rural area, not smoking, routinely exercising, sleeping six to eight hours a night, being normal weight, eating fruits and vegetables, and not eating many fatty or sweet foods.[2]

But no matter how proactive we are, we can't keep our brains from changing with age and experiencing bouts of forgetfulness, absentmindedness, or mental fog.

"Umm . . . where did I park the car?"

"That lady looks familiar. . . . What's her name?"

Losing some mental clarity over time is normal. The most common causes are aging, chronic illness, chemical imbalances, medication side effects, substance abuse, medical conditions, nutritional deficiencies, lack of sleep, lack of mental and physical activity, and others. But even with all these risks stacked against us, there are just as many things we can do to counteract them. You're probably already aware of the best-known tips for memory care and even the science behind them. Some are simply common sense while others require knowledge, judgment, and choice. But actually incorporating them into your daily lifestyle is easier said than done. Procrastination and apathy can set in quickly.

It may help to have an accountability partner like a family member or friend to keep you motivated. Trust me, the short- and especially the long-term benefits are worth the effort.

Start now. Sometimes later becomes never.

Get Enough Uninterrupted Sleep

Insomnia in mid- to late life can be a serious problem. The brain generates about as much energy as a small light-bulb even during sleep, and it needs uninterrupted sleep to recuperate. Doctors often hear, "I can't sleep. Can you help me?" If you or a family member has sleep difficulties, you're not alone. About one-third of the population reports insomnia symptoms, including problems falling asleep and staying asleep. Having nonrestorative sleep can lead to daytime dysfunction.

Check the following activities that you will try for improving your quality of sleep:

_____ Avoid long-term use of sleep aid medications because they may disturb stage IV sleep, making sleep less productive.[3]

_____ Set a regular sleep routine for bedtime and wake-up time.

_____ Reduce light, noise, and stimulating activities one to two hours before bed.

_____ Avoid drinking caffeine and alcohol or eating in the four hours before bedtime.

_____ Eliminate or reduce/shorten daytime naps.

_____ Exercise early in the day because it releases energy-boosting adrenaline.

_____ Clear your mind of worries.

_____ Use a fan for white noise.

_____ Read a relaxing novel or listen to music to get sleepy.

_____ Relax by taking a warm shower or bath. It can stimulate blood flow, so give yourself an hour before bed.

_____ Have a warm, decaffeinated, sugarless drink just before bedtime. (It draws blood to the stomach, causing a sleep sensation because of the slightly decreased blood flow to parts of the brain.)

_____ Check your medications for sleep-related side effects.

Decrease Stress and Blood Pressure

Severe, ongoing stress and/or hypertension (high blood pressure) can contribute to cognitive slowing and dementia. Medication may be necessary also, but the lifestyle changes in this chapter can help control the everyday levels of stress.

Exercise Physically to Get a Boost Mentally

- An active lifestyle increases the brain volume. It has been well documented that aerobic activity is a powerful stimulus for generating structural changes in the brain.

- Physical exercise increases oxygen in the bloodstream and pumps it to the brain. Oxygen is fuel for the brain and helps increase neuron activity.

- Regular exercise releases endorphins, which are natural painkillers and mood boosters, and it burns off toxic chemicals caused by stress.

A good way to kick all of this into action is to schedule yourself a break in your daily routine. For instance, climb stairs at the office or take a walk around the block with the dog or a child. Having someone join you makes it more fun.

Contrary to what many people believe, strenuous workouts aren't necessary to get the benefits of exercise or motion. Research confirms that thirty minutes of moderate activity like walking or cycling three or more times a week is preferable to working out for three hours just once a week. Other aerobic exercises are cardio machines, swimming, hiking, taking exercise classes, or dancing.

Start each day with my quick "7 × 7" wake-up routine:

7 push-ups (on your knees, if you need to)
7 sit-ups/crunches
7 straight leg lefts
7 side leg lifts

7 chest expansions (pull arms back)

7 neck stretches forward and backward

7 full body folds to touch the floor (or your toes)

Consider a Mediterranean Diet and Maintain a Healthy Weight

Everything you eat drugs your brain for good or bad so be careful what you put in your mouth.

Do you or a family member struggle with being overweight? Studies show that a body mass index (BMI) greater than twenty-five may decrease memory. The BMI is a calculated ratio of a person's height and weight. Go online for BMI charts or calculators to get your number. If you are extremely muscular, this number may be skewed higher, but it is a good gauge.

Eat less. It can't get any simpler than that. Portion size is important because mental focus is impacted by eating too much as well as too little. Use smaller plates and bowls, use doggy bags from restaurants, and enjoy every bite. A standard recommendation is to eat until you are 80 percent full. Another hint—avoid extremely low-carb diets because the brain needs a steady flow of carbohydrates to fuel it twenty-four hours a day. Do eat some protein at every meal and decrease obvious and hidden sugars (in prepackaged foods).

Eating breakfast has benefits. Some people skip breakfast to avoid the calories. But eating breakfast is a good foundation for a productive day at any age. For example, the USDA's School Breakfast Program helps foster success in the classroom and healthy lifetime habits. Research supports the claims that breakfast helps improve attention, problem-solving ability, and memory.

Eating well in general contributes to brain longevity as well as short-term benefits like learning and concentration.

I'm especially concerned about the elderly because they typically have poor eating habits, for many reasons. The brain requires certain nutrients and vitamins, so malnutrition makes this population even more vulnerable to mental decline and diseases. Keep this in mind when you visit a senior. Instead of taking flowers and candy, take them a little word-search book, a fun magazine to read, or fresh blueberries.

Wise diet choices include foods high in omega-3 fatty acids or B and D vitamins, plant-derived foods, the spice turmeric, and of course all the other healthy foods you know you should be eating. You can do an online search for specific food lists and sample menus.

Try the Mediterranean diet. Research has proven that people who eat more produce, fish, whole grains, and healthy fats not only weigh less but also have a decreased risk for heart disease, depression, and dementia.

Consider the following foods as a general guideline and make adjustments for your individual preferences. These smart-choice foods are relatively low-cost, widely available, and delicious. A basic rule: If it's white (potatoes, bread), eat less; if it's green, eat more. By making just one or two of the following diet changes, your brain will gain health.[4]

- more fish (omega-3 fatty acids)
- more vegetables (especially yellow and leafy greens)
- baked or grilled chicken and turkey

- tea and coffee in moderation
- more whole grains
- fruits (berries and those with edible skins) for fiber
- more legumes (peas, beans) and nuts (almonds)
- herbs and spices (instead of salt) to flavor foods
- coconut or olive oil (not saturated fats) for cooking to improve levels of good (HDL) cholesterol
- less cheese; choose low-fat dairy products
- less beef and pork
- less cakes, pies, and cookies; avoid simple sugars
- less fried foods
- not skipping meals (skipping meals causes your body to convert food into fat and slows metabolism)

Consider Vitamin Supplements and Antioxidants

It's a good idea to become familiar with omega-3 fatty acids, the B family of vitamins, vitamin D, and antioxidants. In general, vitamins don't hurt—they may even help in many situations. But beware of excessive use of any vitamin. A quality daily multiple vitamin supplement is probably a good idea for people who don't and can't keep up with a well-balanced daily diet.[5]

Be aware: Don't fall for health-food gimmicks that megavitamins touted to be "natural" are better than those synthesized in labs. A vitamin is a chemical—a chemical used in a particular biochemical reaction. It doesn't make any difference whether that chemical has been extracted naturally or synthesized in a lab.

Sometimes supplements are needed—for example, iron for anemia and vitamin D if a person does not get enough sun exposure for the body to make the vitamin (or if a person is otherwise deficient in vitamin D, as is a large part of the population).

Antioxidants can help lower disease-causing free radicals (oxidants) in the brain and elsewhere in the body. This can prevent or stop cell damage caused by chemically unstable oxidants. These are waste products from normal cell functions like metabolism (using food for energy) and from external toxins like pollution, tobacco smoke, and alcohol. Oxidation in cells alters the chemical structure and a cell's function. Incidentally, once a person has significant dementia or Alzheimer's disease, it may be too late for antioxidants to help because these patients metabolize oxygen differently.

The studies on the benefits of antioxidant supplements are conflicted, so discuss these with a medical doctor. Here are a few to consider: fish oil (enteric coated), NAC (N-acetylcysteine), ALA (alpha lipoic acid), and vitamins C, E, D_3, and B complex.

Vitamin B_6 and B_{12} supplements might help in neurogenesis/nerve cell regeneration. B_9 is a memory neurotransmitter.

Foods such as pomegranates, mangoes, blueberries, cherries, red grapes, whey protein, green tea, curry, and turmeric are high in antioxidants.

Drink Alcohol in Moderation and Stay Smoke-Free

Every time you reach for an addictive drug, stop and picture yourself nonfunctioning in a nursing home. It's not worth doing things that damage your brain. Tobacco and alcohol affect the body's ability to deliver oxygen and nutrients to the brain. They speed up the natural aging process and contribute to the formation of brain cell plaques that lead to dementia. Nicotine may temporarily increase neurocognitive functioning, attention, and working memory, but an addiction to nicotine can kill.

Alcohol is one of the most common drugs of abuse. A dependency can decrease life span by fifteen years and has been linked to health problems including almost all types of cognitive decline and dementia. Over time, it will lower brain volume and cause significant physical, psychological, and social consequences.

Some studies suggest that one drink a day for women and two drinks for men may reduce the risk of heart disease and dementia in older adults. I don't recommend taking up drinking alcoholic beverages, but low-dose consumption of certain types may be beneficial.

Get Health Checkups

Regular medical checkups from a family physician or internist are especially important for people over age fifty. If problems can be identified and treated in the early stages, they have a better chance of being stopped or cured. Make a note to discuss any memory concerns at your next healthcare appointment.

Have the doctor review all your prescription medications and over-the-counter drugs. Older people metabolize medications at a slower rate and can reach toxic levels easier than younger adults. This combined with side effects and drug interactions can cause changes in mood, confusion, and memory loss.

Socialize

We all have a core need to be loved and accepted; support is one of the single most important psychological needs. Remind yourself every day that *relationships are more important than projects*. This truth may disrupt some of your routines or thought patterns, but it's for the good.

It has been said that a burden shared is only half a burden. We all need people to talk to. Spending time with family and friends engages areas of the brain that process attention, memory, and cognitive tasks. Make an effort to reach out to someone you know who may be lonely; it'll be good for both of you. And don't overlook your sibling relationships. Those natural bonds may need to be revived and nurtured.

Protect Your Head from Jolts and Bumps

Always wear a seatbelt, use a helmet for sports, and fallproof your home. Even relatively mild head injuries can cause emotional, behavioral, and cognitive changes.

Brain injuries occur when the head is hit hard enough to cause the brain to move suddenly within the skull, usually from a shaking movement or violent impact with something. This can cause a contusion (bruise) on the brain, hemorrhage (bleeding) within it, or a concussion (a traumatic brain injury with a functional change). If the damage is severe, it can even cause shearing injuries to nerve fibers and neurons.

All concussion brain injuries are serious. A direct blow to the face, head, neck, or anywhere else on the body with a force transmitted to the head can make you "see stars" or "ring your bell."

Concussions are graded with clinical symptoms: (1) presence or absence of loss of consciousness, (2) duration of loss of consciousness, (3) duration of post-traumatic memory loss, and (4) persistence of symptoms, including headache, dizziness, lack of concentration, and so on. For people who sustain severe injury to the brain and are in a coma (comatose is a state of unconsciousness), recovery is variable.

Watch for these symptoms:

- a short-lived impairment of neurological function
- constant or recurring headache
- inability to control motor functions or balance; dizziness
- changes in ability to hear, taste, or see
- hypersensitivity to light or sound
- shortened attention span; easily distracted; over-stimulated by environment
- difficulty staying focused on a task, following directions, or understanding information
- feeling of disorientation and confusion and other neuropsychological deficiencies
- difficulty expressing words or thoughts

Adults at play are also at risk. Cerebral concussions are all too common for the young and for middle-aged adults who enjoy recreational sports on weekends and during vacations.

They are especially at risk if they're tired or not feeling well or are under the influence of alcohol or drugs. Also, they may not wear the appropriate gear and follow all safety rules.

Warning: Helmets aren't just for kids. Adults need to use protective headgear for cycling, football, baseball, softball, horseback riding, ice and roller hockey, martial arts, roller and inline skating, rugby, and lacrosse, just to name a few. They're also needed for riding off-road recreational vehicles (ATVs, dune buggies, go-carts, minibikes) and for winter sports (snow skiing, sledding, snowboarding, snowmobiling, and ice skating).

Concussions can happen on the water too. Even at slow speeds, a skier or someone riding behind a boat on an inner tube can get a concussion when they hit the water. It's a matter of how a person lands. Diving, scuba diving, surfing, swimming, wakeboarding, water polo, water skiing, and tubing all have risks.

Adult "weekend warriors" need to be especially careful on backyard trampolines because of the dangers of landing on the head and neck from different angles.

The main treatment for a concussion is rest and sleep. Brain (cognitive) rest and physical rest allow time for the brain to heal. It may take days, weeks, or months. Concussions impact the brain's cognitive (mental) functions (thinking, concentrating, learning, and reasoning), so cognitive activities may make symptoms worse and extend the recovery time.

Cognitive rest means time off from work and limiting visual stimulants, such as television, computers, video games, texts, and cell phones. Reading, exercising, physical exertion causing perspiration, and trips out of the home also need to be limited or avoided.

Certain types of head injuries may actually increase the risk of a person developing Alzheimer's disease or other dementias later in life. The greatest increase in future dementia risk seems to occur after a severe head injury that knocks a person unconscious or repeated head traumas; damaged tissue doesn't hold up well to further injuries.

The effects of multiple or repetitive concussions are currently being studied by researchers around the world. Professional athletes are at increased risk of developing mild cognitive impairment, chronic traumatic encephalopathy, postconcussion syndrome, and other long-term consequences. It's crucial that a person fully recover from one concussion before risking another one to avoid further neurologic damage.

Note: While concussions can happen at any age, any brain injuries in children warrant specialized assessment and approaches to intervention. Recognizing concussions in children can be complicated since a child may not be capable of describing the more subjective symptoms, such as feeling in a fog or vertigo. Some symptoms, including irritability, may be mistaken as a behavioral issue rather than a sign of a brain injury. Some postconcussion symptoms affect higher-level cognitive processes, which a young child may not yet be using.

Children are generally resilient, and plasticity—the ability of the brain to reorganize itself and form new connections—is generally at its strongest in childhood. Most children recover from a concussion. Mental and physical rest is encouraged, but complete inactivity is not recommended.

Give Your Mind Results-Driven Workouts

In time, failing to challenge your brain can result in cerebral atrophy, or shrinking of the brain. Mental workouts increase the number of connections between nerve cells, which provides a range of ways for cells to communicate with each other and increases the speed with which they do it. Brain cell connections help you stay focused, anticipate and respond appropriately, recall memories, and process new information.

Stimulate your mind every day! This is doable even if you're a little unmotivated: read, play online brain games, do puzzles, practice new skills, play word games, learn something new, engage in hobbies, test your recall, do math in your head, draw things (like maps) from memory, practice hand-eye coordination, and listen to music. Try using your opposite hand for routine chores such as brushing your teeth, buttoning a shirt, tying shoelaces, or writing your name. This strengthens neural connections and even grows new ones. It's like physical exercise that improves body functions and develops muscles.

Having a stimulating environment is also helpful. Pet birds in cages need a variety of challenging and diverse environments for healthy physical and mental stimulation. The same is true for people. Take short car trips or different routes around town for a change of scenery. Meet friends at different places for coffee and conversation. Go to movies and local sporting events and take walks in different parks. Whatever activity you choose, venture out of your comfort zone.

Your Mind Would Be a Terrible Thing to Lose

You're not the only one who needs to take all of this advice seriously. You are in good company. Out of our country's estimated population of over 328,800,000, guess how many other people need to pay more attention to this advice too. All of them! For many, it's a matter of life and death, or certainly quality of life. Now it's also a matter of choice.

Note: This information is not intended as a specific guide for any treatment; one's medical doctor should be consulted for any and all medical advice. Any specifics given here only make general reference to treatments that may have been tried in the past. Even the dos and don'ts are not necessarily absolute; individual variations might exist.

Choose Well

What's Your Action Plan?

To make a difference in your long-term mental ability, you'll need to do more than just sporadically tweak a routine. You'll need a plan that will not only specifically list what you want to change but also determine when, where, and how you're going to do it. Committing to these behavioral changes will make a big difference. The best way to get something done is to begin.

Check what you will commit to now:

_____ fight procrastination ("I'll start after . . . ; it's not that important; I'm too busy right now.")

_____ read food labels at the grocery store—nutrition information and ingredients lists; look for three or more grams of whole-grain fiber, less than 5 percent sodium, and protein (*Red flag*: when first ingredients are sugar or aliases, refined grain, trans fats, or chemical additives)

_____ simplify your routines and prioritize your activities to decrease stress

_____ improve your sleep habits

_____ start eating more of the Mediterranean diet

_____ decrease caffeine and alcohol

_____ revive a special interest

_____ figure your body mass index (BMI)

_____ check your medications' product information for side effects

_____ try the 7 x 7 wake-up exercises

_____ consider vitamin and antioxidant needs

_____ schedule a health checkup with your doctor

_____ use your nondominant hand for everything you can

_____ don't go to bed hungry or after overeating

_____ reread Choose Well sections from this book

_____ vary your exercise routine

_____ exercise gently to moderately twenty to thirty minutes every day

_____ schedule social outings with family or friends

_____ eat more lean protein and less sugar

_____ read something every day (magazine, newspaper)

____ avoid boredom

____ review Brain Boosters exercises in this book

____ eat "rainbow" foods—orange, red, blue, purple, and green

____ learn how to do something new

____ identify one thing that's stressful in your life and make a plan to address it

Try this plan for a week or two. If it isn't working for you after that stint, choose other options and make adjustments— but don't quit. At least you're off dead center and are doing something!

Brain Boosters

Famous People in History

Are the following facts about these famous people in history correct? Even one incorrect entry renders a false answer for the entire chart.

	Adam and Eve, first man and woman
470–399 BC	Socrates, a classical Greek philosopher
460–370 BC	Hippocrates, a Greek physician
428–348 BC	Plato, student of Socrates and teacher of Aristotle
384–322 BC	Aristotle taught Alexander the Great
69–30 BC	Cleopatra, the last active pharaoh of Ptolemaic Egypt
5 BC–AD 33	Jesus Christ, the central figure of Christianity
1492	Christopher Columbus discovered America
1776	Thomas Jefferson and the Declaration of Independence

1905	Einstein and E=MC^2
1969	man walked on the moon—Apollo 11
1981–89	Ronald Reagan served as president of the United States
2009	Barack Obama inaugurated as president of the United States

True (correct) _____   False (incorrect) _____

Math Concepts

Knowing a math concept means you know the workings behind the answer. Because you know why things work, you can figure out the answers and formulas yourself. This allows you to think and process abstractly.

Are the following mathematical concepts defined correctly? Even one inaccuracy renders the entire statement incorrect/false.

			True	False
1. algebra	a mathematical system that solves arithmetic problems through the use of letters to stand for numbers		_____	_____
2. geometry	a mathematical system involving relationships of points, lines, planes, and solids		_____	_____
3. trigonometry	angles of triangles		_____	_____
4. abscissa	x is the horizontal distance of a point from a vertical scale		_____	_____
5. ordinate	y is the vertical distance of a point from a horizontal scale		_____	_____
6. integers	whole numbers both positive and negative		_____	_____

		True	False
7. prime number	divisible only by 1 and the number itself	____	____
8. right angle	an angle of 90 degrees	____	____
9. distance	= rate x time; d = rt	____	____
10. hypotenuse	the longest side of a right triangle; the side opposite the 90 degree angle	____	____
11. Pi(Π)	the ratio between the circumference of a circle and its diameter; Π = 3.1416; Π = c/d = circumference/diameter	____	____

Biology Definitions

Biology is the study of life and living organisms (origins, growth, reproduction, structure, and behavior), from one-celled creatures to the most complex living organism of all, the human being. It includes the study of genes and cells that give living things their special characteristics.

Are all the following biology definitions and concepts correct?

		True	False
1. biology	the study of living organisms	____	____
2. acids	chemical compounds that release hydrogen ions in solution	____	____
3. bases	chemical compounds that accept hydrogen ions in solution	____	____
4. nucleic acids	large molecules that contain the genetic code for that organism	____	____
5. cytoplasm	a semiliquid substance that contains organelles	____	____

179

		True	False
6. organelles	microscopic bodies within the cytoplasm that perform distinct functions	___	___
7. ribosomes	organelle bodies bound to the endoplasmic reticulum that are the sites of protein synthesis	___	___
8. Golgi	an organelle that is the site of protein and apparatus lipid processing	___	___
9. enzymes	proteins that catalyze chemical reactions within cells	___	___
10. mitochondria	the organelle that is the site of energy production within cells	___	___
11. nucleus	the organelle that contains the genetic material DNA	___	___
12. diffusion	the movement of molecules from a region of higher concentration to one of lower concentration	___	___
13. osmosis	diffusion involving only water molecules and often across a semipermeable membrane	___	___
14. adenosine	the chemical that provides the energy in cells' triphosphate (ATP)	___	___
15. photosynthesis	the process in plants of utilizing energy to synthesize carbohydrates	___	___
16. Krebs cycle	the subdivision of cellular respiration in which pyruvic acid is broken down and the resulting energy is used to form high-energy compounds	___	___
17. mitosis	a type of cell division occurring in phases that results in two daughter cells each with the same number and kind of chromosomes as the parent cell; the process by which cells reproduce	___	___

		True	False
18. meiosis	a type of cell division by which the chromosome number is halved during gamete formation; the process by which sperm cells and egg cells are produced	____	____
19. genome	the set of all genes that specify an organism's traits	____	____
20. genotype	the gene composition of a living organism	____	____
21. phenotype	the expression of the genes of a living organism	____	____
22. taxonomy	the science of classification of organisms	____	____
23. invertebrates	animals with no backbones, such as sponges, jellyfish, tapeworms, roundworms, earthworms, snails, squids, oysters, octopuses, spiders, ticks, lobsters, insects, sea urchins, and some reptiles	____	____
24. vertebrates	animals with backbones, such as fish, amphibians, some reptiles, birds, and mammals	____	____

9

Homework for Life

IT'S A FACT: Lifelong learning is not only fun, it also stimulates memory and cognitive abilities by engaging the brain's visual, attention, emotion, logic, instinct, muscle, and language centers. At all ages, the brain likes new information, novelty, and variety. Give it what it wants.

The goal is to match our "brain spans" to our life spans, so we can live more fully to the end.

When was the last time you studied for a certification test, memorized remarks for a presentation, took a class, or did some kind of intellectual work? A good memory can save you time, give you an edge at work, and even make you more likeable if you remember people's names and personal details. Life takes homework.

Improving memory skills is important no matter what your age. Your memory may determine career advancements, what your financial future holds, and even how well your mind serves you through your adulthood and into old age.

I know firsthand that the brain can be trained, developed, and improved at any age. In the sixth grade I was near the bottom of my class. I became nervous taking tests, and one day a test grade put me at rock bottom. In the seventh grade, for some reason unknown to me, a teacher, Mr. Gary Baily, awarded me the "outstanding math student." It inspired me to work harder. In the eighth grade I began to compete with Alice Mayfield for top position going into high school. The competition was a kind and healthy one. I studied every night until 10:00 p.m. We were covaledictorians. My confidence was building as I headed to college.

I became a lifelong learner using formal and informal opportunities for personal fulfillment. When I turned sixty I decided to see how I would perform on the Miller Analogy Test (MAT). The MAT is a test for graduate school applicants, with difficult analogies. I scored in the top 1 percent. I also joined American Mensa at age sixty. How did I do it? I followed the steps I'm sharing with you here.

I admit these are traditional approaches to learning and that other techniques may be more aligned with the current technological environment, but these methods worked for me. They are based on rote learning and memorization. Some educational reformers support more progressive practices that focus on student-centered needs, self-control, and task-based approaches to learning. However, standardized testing still favors the more traditional approach.[1]

The Economics of Learning

Aristotle said, "Education is the provision for old age." He was right because education not only sets you up for more financial stability but also helps preserve the brain.

There are ongoing debates around kitchen tables and in business meetings about the value of a college degree. Considering the investments of time and money involved, some skeptics wonder if the returns of college are worth the costs. However, it's well documented that college graduates earn more than those with less education. College degrees may not guarantee higher income, but they come closer than just about any other investment one can make.[2]

Earnings generally increase with the number of years spent in school; higher education equates to future financial benefits. According to the 2015 US Bureau of Labor Statistics, without a high school diploma, a person's average weekly earnings are $493, which is $25,636 per year. A high school graduate averages $678 a week, and $798 is expected with an associate's degree. A bachelor's degree brings average earnings of $1,137 per week ($59,124 a year), and a master's level graduate earns on average $1,341 weekly. Doctoral salaries are higher ($1,700+). But be aware that these education-based salaries can vary greatly depending on different regions of the country, years of experience, occupational fields, and other factors.[3]

Going through about twenty-six years of school (grade school, junior high, high school, college, medical school, rotating internships, psychiatry residency, board certifications, seminary, and PhD), I used the following learning techniques. They also helped me excel on tests for American

Mensa and the American Society of Clinical Psychopharmacology in my senior years. They have served me well.

But education isn't the only ticket to success. There should be even more effort invested in developing personal qualities that will serve you well no matter what paths you take throughout life: self-discipline, social skills, work ethic, willpower, drive, patience, accountability, integrity, optimism, self-confidence, communication, honesty, commitment, and, of course, being a continuous learner.

What's Your Natural Learning Style?

Would you rather have someone show you how to do something, be told how to do it, or just do it yourself through trial and error? When you have to pick up a few things from the drugstore, do you make a written list, repeat them in your head a few times, or use your fingers to name each item?

People learn differently. Some learn best by hearing information (*auditory*). Others respond more to seeing information (*visual*), and others learn by using their hands (*tactile*). Some people learn well in groups while others prefer studying alone. Some like to move around as they study; others prefer to sit still.

Some people naturally organize their thoughts and experiences in particular learning categories: verbal/linguistics, logical, mathematical, musical, visual/spatial, body/kinesthetic, and interpersonal characteristics.

When children are young, parents may notice a child's natural learning tendencies. This is helpful for homework assignments and teaching skills at home. But I suggest blending and developing all of these styles.

For a person with dementia, the sense of touch (tactile) can trigger memories in ways other forms of communication can't. Touching special items can stimulate their memories. Think what items may hold special significance for the person. Did they play a sport or an instrument? Did they spend a lot of time in the kitchen, in the garden, or in a workshop? Then collect the items so they're easy to pull out when that person needs to be calmed or comforted. Designate a "memory box" or a shelf or drawer.[4]

Tips to Boost Your "Mental Homework" Time

If you're finding it more and more difficult to remember things or you want to boost your memory power, consider the following tips and work them into your routines.

- Determine your *best biological time of day*. Are you sharper in the early morning or late at night? Use these personal peak times for reading, paperwork, and mind games.
- Use your time wisely. Find *spare moments* each day for mental exercise. I studied countless hours but in bits of time by carrying around summary cards and pages of my notes—a moment here and a moment there. You'll find more of these moments if you watch for them and simplify your routines and tasks. I used spare moments to write about fifty books.

- For big learning projects, break them down into *small parts*. Notice how books are divided into chapters. If you read one chapter each day, you'll soon complete the whole book.

- Have *organized places* to read and study, with a comfortable chair and good lighting. Declutter these "thinking" areas.

- Take *short breaks* every twenty to thirty minutes. Walk around, stretch, get something to drink, or step outside for some fresh air. This helps you stay alert.

- Keep *clocks and calendars* in the rooms where you spend the most time.

- Keep a *smartphone or notebook* handy to keep track of names, phone numbers, appointments, lists, errands, addresses and directions, and so on.

- It's easy to lose track of time. Set *alarms* for important things you need to do. Put *sticky notes* around the house as reminders to do important things you might forget.

- If you want to remember something, *say it aloud*— several times. I often do this when I'm driving alone in the car.

- Before going to bed, decide on the three *most important tasks* for the next day and write them down. Doing so will get each new day off to a good start.

- Make mental homework a *priority*.

Practice Memory Techniques

There are many memory techniques—mnemonics are systems for improving and assisting the memory. They help us remember information.

The most common types are music (lyrics and tunes), name (first letter in each word for a list of items), expression/word (first letter of each item in a list to form a phrase or word), model (pie charts, sequence or pyramid models), ode (in the form of a poem or rhyme), note organization (notecards, outlines, questions and answers), image (pictures that promote recall of information), connection (information connected to something already known), and spelling (splitting words into smaller words or letter combinations).[5]

You probably already use some of these techniques without even realizing it. Try as many as you can, and choose the ones that work best for you.

Visualization with exaggeration and linking helps vocabulary and improves short-term memory. Examples:

Visualize interesting *synonyms* for the word *big*: Imagine you are strolling down the beach when you see an enormous ship. Your mind sees a myriad of (many) people boarding the ship. The boat is capacious (roomy). The ship is headed to a megalopolis (you have a friend named Meg who lives in the city, so you can link to megalopolis).

Visualize and link a *list of items*: You need to buy milk, coconuts, bananas, and bread. Visualize a monkey swinging through the trees (coconut and banana trees). The coconut has milk in it, and you know a great banana bread recipe.

Now you've linked in your mind all of the objects you need to buy.

Use *exaggerations* or funny sentences for recall. Example:

To remember a person by the name of Longman, visualize a man who is very long or tall; exaggerate it in your mind.

Use *associations* by connecting new information with old (common) information. Examples:

The music treble clef (E, G, B, D, F) is recalled with, "Every Good Boy Does Fine."

In geography, Italy is easily remembered by many because it is shaped like a boot.

When using a screwdriver or faucet, think of "lefty loosey, righty tighty."

Acronyms are formed from the initial letters of other words and pronounced as a word. Example:

In medical school I learned the symptoms of dementia with "IMAJO" (meaning impairment in Intellect, Memory, Affect, Judgment, and Orientation).

My Easy Learning Plan

When studying a chapter in a book or a group of notes, follow these three steps:

1. First, skim the material as quickly as possible.
2. Then read it through slowly. (Read important parts out loud to help you remember.)
3. Finally, study the material and write down a brief outline for review.

This is how the plan works as a one-hour study session:

- Preview, two minutes. Quickly preview the chapter titles, subtitles, and paragraph titles of the entire chapter.
- Skim, eight minutes. Rapidly read the chapter.
- Break, two minutes. Take a quick break and do ten push-ups or just walk around.
- Read, thirty-three minutes. Read the material more slowly this time.
- Break, five minutes. Take a little longer break so you are able to concentrate better.
- Study, ten minutes. Make a brief outline and commit what you can to memory.

Test-Taking Tips

Some readers may be preparing for a professional certification, job promotion exam, or admission to a career enhancement program. Good luck to everyone with exams, especially those who are reading this instead of studying.

Others may be long past having to take exams. If this isn't currently relevant to you, please share it with your children or grandchildren to show you're interested in their education and success.

These easy tips may help you prepare and do your best the day of the test:

- Knowledge is the best strategy. *Read the material several times*. Repetition is the key to learning.
- *Take good notes* for review. I always figured that instructors would ask on the test what they had put time into teaching and discussing in class, and I was right. In medical school I summarized each page of lecture notes. On the back of that page I listed the top three points, and quickly reviewed them daily.

  An outline format is easier to study. Put three subpoints under each of the three key points.

  Use patterns of threes, fours, or fives and no more than sevens for your notes. The brain has trouble recalling more than seven. Think of phone numbers: many people can repeat and remember a seven-digit phone number, but if you have to include an unfamiliar area code also, ten numbers becomes harder to remember without writing them down.

- *Take as many pretests* as possible. Familiarity with the format can increase a score substantially. Use different but similar tests that were either used in the past or prepared for study.

- *Practice relaxation* for a few days before. Breathe in and out slowly and then relax. Tell yourself you can do this. In other words, marshal the brain to produce for you.

- *Stop studying one hour before bedtime the night before the test.* Let your brain relax and consolidate for recall what you've learned.
- *Be well rested the day of the test.* The brain needs to be at its best—rested, quick, sharp. Go to bed early the night before the test.
- *Drink one cup of coffee that morning.* A reasonable dose of caffeine results in more dopamine in the brain, and more dopamine increases focus, efficiency, and memory.
- *Put every issue except the test out of your mind* for one hour before and remain that way until the test is over. Don't let your mind stray. A divided mind is an inefficient mind.
- Because of the extra power of short-term memory, *cram* (really focus and study extra) in the few days prior to the test (but be reasonable). However, cramming can't replace learning in bite-sized bits throughout the course.
- *Go to the test site early* so as not to feel rushed.
- *Keep track of time.* Time is a factor on many tests.
- *Read directions carefully.* This is often overlooked and is very important.
- *Read every question carefully.* Trick questions are sometimes present. Many questions are missed because of a lack of reading the entire question.
- *Know the type of test questions* (essay or objective specifics), and prepare accordingly.

- *Write neatly and use impressive vocabulary* in essay questions. Arrange your answer systematically with three subpoints under any major point. An occasional less-well-known vocabulary word improves your answer.
- In *objective-type tests*, "all of the above" is more likely to be a better choice than "none of the above."
- For *true-false questions*, "all," "never," and "always" questions are often false. When *general terms* are used ("most," "some," "usually," and "might"), true is usually the better answer.
- For *multiple-choice questions* in which two of four answers are opposites, one of the opposites is often the right answer.
- *The 60 percent rule*: play the odds when not sure of the correct answer. In multiple-choice tests, rule out any answers you feel are false with a 60 percent certainty.
- The *order of probability* on many tests is C. B. A. D., but never make random selections. Rule out at least one or two of the choices if you can.
- *Take your best guess early*. Answer every question as you go. Your first answer is often the best answer. If you feel you were nervous early in the test and this decreased your reasoning (or if you see facts within questions later in the test that help you know the answer to a previous question), go back and change an answer if you have more than 60 percent certainty in the change.

When all else fails and superstition takes over, resort to using your lucky pen. This reminds me of the *Gomer Pyle, USMC*

TV comedy series in the 1960s. There is a hilarious episode in which Sgt. Carter and Gomer Pyle are both taking an exam to be officer candidates. It's a true/false test, and Gomer keeps whacking two fingers on the desk. One finger is true and the other is false—whichever hurts most after the whack is the answer he writes down. He calls it "hunching." Sgt. Carter is distracted by the noise, and Gomer scores higher.

Choose Well

Self-Assessment: Are You a Lifelong Learner?

Lifelong learning is deliberate and voluntary. It's having a positive attitude toward personal and career opportunities. It can boost your confidence and self-esteem, make you less risk averse and more adaptable to change, help you enjoy a more satisfying personal life, and be fun.

Do you . . .	Yes	No
believe you can keep your mind sharp?		
experience any mental decline?		
use your spare time wisely?		
know your natural learning style?		
use any memory techniques?		
want to improve your reading skills?		
have interest in improving your vocabulary?		
have the willpower to exercise your brain?		
have a clear life purpose?		
need to make any lifestyle changes?		

Do you...	Yes	No
take advantage of workplace training?	_____	_____
have any learning projects underway?	_____	_____

Make a plan to address any of these questions that concern you. It may just mean making a few modifications. It doesn't have to be complicated.

Brain Boosters

Because the brain can develop the more it's exercised, it can be compared to muscles. Brain development with quick cognition is beneficial to all aspects of your life, just as a fit body is.

Pictures on Coins and Bills

The US Treasury announced in 2016 the twenty-dollar bill will feature Harriet Tubman on the front, with Andrew Jackson and an image of the White House on the back. The new five-dollar and ten-dollar bills will feature women and civil rights leaders on the back. The designs will be unveiled in 2020, but the circulation date has yet to be released.

Whose pictures are on US coins and bills? Are all of the following correct?

Coin or Bill	Picture	True	False
1. one cent/penny	Lincoln	_____	_____
2. five cents/nickel	Jefferson	_____	_____
3. ten cents/dime	Roosevelt	_____	_____

Coin or Bill	Picture	True	False
4. twenty-five cents/ quarter	Washington	____	____
5. one-dollar bill	Washington	____	____
6. five-dollar bill	Lincoln	____	____
7. ten-dollar bill	Hamilton	____	____
8. twenty-dollar bill	Jackson	____	____
9. fifty-dollar bill	Reagan	____	____
10. one-hundred-dollar bill	Franklin	____	____

Functions of the Mind

Psychology is the study of how the human mind functions, including the attitude, behavior, thinking, and reasoning of who we are. Naturally, it includes how to improve memory.

Are the following statements correct (true) or incorrect (false)?

	True	False
1. Memory is stored in vocabulary, concepts (knowledge), and visualization. A photographic memory can be developed to a degree through practice.	____	____
2. Neuroplasticity refers to the lifelong capacity of the brain to change and rewire itself in response to the stimulation of learning and experience.	____	____
3. The subconscious mind is like a memory bank with a virtually unlimited capacity. It permanently stores everything that ever happens to you.	____	____
4. Thinking involves the mediation of ideas or data when we form concepts and engage in problem solving, reasoning, and decision making.	____	____

| | True | False |

5. The mind is a set of cognitive faculties including consciousness, perception, thinking, judgment, and memory.

6. Cognition includes perception, attention, working memory, long-term memory, producing and understanding language, learning, reasoning, problem solving, and decision making.

7. Social psychology studies how humans think about and relate to each other.

8. Personality deals with patterns of behavior, thought, and emotion in individuals.

9. Developmental psychology seeks to understand how people come to perceive, understand, and act and how these processes change as they age.

10. Educational psychology studies how we learn in educational settings, the effectiveness of educational interventions, and the psychology of teaching.

English

Learning reading, spelling, literature, and composition develops our comprehension and use of the written and oral language.

Are the following concepts defined correctly?[6]

		True	False
1. noun	a part of speech that names a person, place, or thing		
2. verb	a part of speech that indicates an action		

		True	False
3. pronoun	a word that replaces a noun	___	___
4. tense	a form taken by a verb to indicate the time of action, such as present, past, future, present perfect, past perfect, and future perfect	___	___
5. indicative mood	a verb form that makes a statement	___	___
6. imperative mood	a verb form that expresses a command	___	___
7. adjective	a part of speech that modifies a verb, an adjective, or an adverb	___	___
8. adverb	a part of speech that modifies a noun	___	___
9. preposition	a part of speech that connects, such as *at, through, by, on, across, for, like, with,* and *to*	___	___
10. conjunction	a joining word that links parts of sentences, such as *and* or *but*	___	___

10

Mental Exercise with Words

IT'S A FACT: We think in words. We communicate in words. Memory is largely stored in words. Thoughts become words, and words become actions.

Some words are just plain fun to say. Read the following aloud and enjoy:

ballyhoo (sensational publicity)
cattywampus (in disarray)
collywobbles (bellyache)
flibbertigibbet (frivolous, flighty person)
gobbledygook (unclear, wordy jargon)
hootenanny (informal folk performance)
itty-bitty (very small)
lollygag (waste time in aimless activity)
namby-pamby (weak, indecisive person)

piffle (nonsense)

snickersnee (long knife)

tintinnabulation (ringing sound of bells)

williwaw (violent gust of cold wind)

zedonk (offspring of a zebra and donkey)

There's Something Special about These Times

It's an unusually fruitful era when it comes to words. You're lucky if you still have teenagers in your life because keeping up with their vocabulary can make you "cool" and exercise your brain at the same time. The trending words, slang, and emojis are continually morphing. Learning this viral language gives your brain a workout.

Many words and phrases have been shortened to abbreviations and acronyms. Tumblr, YouTube, and Twitter are leading this slang game. Try using some of the following when you text your kids or grandkids. It will blow their minds.

KMU—keep me updated

IMU—I miss you

QAP—quick as possible

GLWT—good luck with that

HW—homework

NON—now or never

HYB—how you been?

YDU—you don't understand

IGHT—alright, okay

IDK—I don't know
WUW—what you want?
N/C—not cool

It's also challenging to understand how words that have real meanings aren't always used properly anymore.

Salty—Bitter, upset. Example: "She's really salty she couldn't get the day off yesterday."

Clutch—This term means "cool" or "job well done." Example: "Your kitchen remodel is so clutch."

Fire—Superhot and trendy. Example: "Where did you get those comfy looking shoes? They're fire."

Gucci—Derived from the name of the upscale fashion retailer, this term means "really cool." Example: "Your new stand-up desk? That's Gucci."

But the age-old form of wordless communication hasn't changed: eye rolling.

Yes, words are fun. As a youth, I was fascinated with words and their meanings. I enjoyed reading books and playing word games. In high school I started appreciating the logic and nuances of words. Finding the right words helped me connect with people, a skill I depended on in my years of answering calls on radio and television talk shows. Then as a senior citizen preparing for the Mensa admission test, I often reviewed up to one thousand words a day. The more words I memorized, the more my intellect and rapid reasoning increased. I passed into the top of American Mensa. After age sixty-five, I also became one of 122 in America and Canada to pass for the third time the prestigious exam for the American Society of Clinical Psychopharmacology.

Words can also be inspiring. Love, choice, faith, success, truth, peace, dream, hope, joy, heaven, believe, achieve, respect, beauty, laughter, create, kindness, energy, grateful, spirit, and happy all describe concepts that calm and inspire us.

Words matter. They shape your life. As your vocabulary develops, it becomes a broader foundation for communicating and acquiring further knowledge.

Your Words Become Your World

The limits of my language mean the limits of my world.

Ludwig Wittgenstein, philosopher

Change your language and you change your thoughts.

Karl Albrecht, entrepreneur

Language shapes the way we think and determines what we can think about.

Benjamin Lee Whorf, linguist

Others judge you by how you use words. If you want to be more effective in sharing thoughts and better understand what you hear and read, expand your vocabulary. The size of vocabulary varies greatly from person to person, but it is estimated that people typically use about five to ten thousand words in everyday life. The average adult has a total vocabulary of about ten to twenty thousand words. This includes all the words they recognize or use in reading, listening, speaking, and writing.[1]

But this is just the tip of the iceberg. The number of words in the English language is just over one million, and about fifteen new words are added daily, so there are always new words to learn![2] It would be fun to focus your vocabulary exercises on these new words to impress your friends.

Learn Words for Your Brain's Sake

> One forgets words as one forgets names. One's vocabulary needs constant fertilizing, or it will die.
>
> Evelyn Waugh, writer

To stimulate your memory, I suggest learning or reviewing at least a few new words each day. Every word learned triggers another memory because words and definitions are connected to others. This mental exercise increases brainpower (see appendix C).

Some of the words you've learned about in this book are dementia, cognition, synapses, neurons, willpower, neuroplasticity, genome, impairment, neurogenesis, purpose, memory, and brain connections. Try using them in your mental exercises.

How to learn new words:

- *Read.* The more pleasure reading you do, the better. Most new words are learned from seeing them in a book or magazine. The more words you're exposed to, the better vocabulary you'll have. Reading aloud gives your mental exercise an extra boost.

- *Learn new words* in phrases or in a sentence so you'll remember the context.
- *Pay attention to how words are used*. The context of a new word in a sentence or story is often enough to guess the meaning. You'll pick up vocabulary without even realizing it.
- *Write down words and definitions*, then practice using them in sentences. The more you say them, the better you'll remember.
- *Make up word associations* and connections with pictures or other words.
- *Play with words*. Play Scrabble and Boggle and do crossword puzzles. Many word games are available online and in leisure workbooks.
- *Get in the habit of looking up the definitions* of words you don't know.
- *Repeat*. Research shows that it takes ten to twenty uses or memory repetitions to make a word part of your vocabulary.[3] Seeing and using the word again and again helps you retain it.

A well-developed vocabulary is the outward sign of a well-developed mind. Words are the working tools of your brain, just as surely as your hands or your eyes.

Marilyn vos Savant, author and columnist[4]

Words that are often heard together (such as salt and pepper) or words that share some of their meaning (such as nurse and doctor) are connected or associated in the brain. The following brainteaser will stimulate the connections or associations between words in your brain. You will see pairs of words; the goal is to find a third word that is connected or associated with both of these two words. For example, consider the pair *piano* and *lock*. The answer is *key*. There are *keys* on a piano and you use a *key* to lock doors. *Key* is called a homograph, a word that has more than one meaning but is always spelled the same.

Are you ready to stimulate connections in your brain? What is the homograph for each pair?[5] (See appendix D for the answers.)

1. ship/card =
2. tree/car =
3. school/eye =
4. pillow/court =
5. river/money =
6. bed/paper =
7. army/water =
8. tennis/noise =
9. Egyptian/mother =
10. smoker/plumber =

What Can Make You Smarter and More Successful?

Reading. It's better for your brain than playing on your smartphone while you kill time at airports or relax at home. Personal electronics keep your brain flitting and multitasking throughout the day. But when you read a book, your attention stays focused and steady. Put your smartphone down and read for fifteen to twenty minutes before you go to work or start your day. Your stress level will decrease and your concentration will increase.

Reading can also help you be more successful in anything you do because being well-read, articulate, and knowledgeable in a variety of topics is important in almost every occupation.

Reading

- keeps the memory and learning capacity sharp
- expands vocabulary and improves spelling and communication skills
- develops analytical skills, concentration, and creativity
- encourages positive thinking, empathy, and motivation and boosts self-confidence
- reduces stress and the risk of dementia and Alzheimer's disease
- increases blood flow and stimulates different areas of the brain

It's interesting that the level of mental exercise varies with different types of reading. For instance, reading a novel for literary study exercises more complex cognitive functions than pleasure reading. The more difficult the reading, the greater the benefits.

Reading changes the brain. Not everyone is a good reader, but poor readers can be trained, which changes and boosts their brain structure. Reading is a complex process involving different centers of the brain working together to increase the connectivity between various neural circuits. For example, the cerebrum interprets vision and hearing, speech, emotions, learning, and fine movement. Language, memory, problem solving, judgment, and reasoning are managed in the frontal lobes. The left temporal cortex is associated with receptivity for language. And the angular and supramarginal gyrus link these parts of the brain together to execute reading.

Get something good to read. There are enough reading categories to interest everyone throughout their lifetime: fiction, nonfiction, biographies, self-help, hobbies, travel, science fiction, history, youth, resources, guides, mysteries, classical literature, satires, anthologies, religion, and more. Books entertain and help us understand different cultures and societies, and they relate history and concepts to today's world.

Get a free library card from your local library or download some ebooks. It may take a week or so to get used to an e-reader, but your brain will adapt. It's fast, easy, inexpensive, and portable. Audiobooks are another good option for car trips and long commutes. When listening to reading or reading aloud, different brain circuits are used than when you read silently to yourself.

One more thing: consider turning off the TV sometimes. Reading is more neurologically demanding. Most television programming doesn't stimulate the brain; that's why it's so relaxing. The brain just processes images and speech, and the visual imagery is automatic. At least choose to watch more educational programs or ones with complex plotlines and characters, so you can engage your brain.

Start Building Your Cognitive Reserve

Because cognitive function peaks in the early thirties, do all you can do to keep your brain fit so you can keep living a vital life for the next four to five decades. Cognition is more than just memorization. It is insight, perception, discernment, comprehension, and learning; it is the process of acquiring knowledge and understanding.

People who have cognitive reserves can be more resistant to age-related brain changes or Alzheimer's disease. They are also less likely to show early signs of dementia, such as short-term memory loss and difficulty multitasking.

At some point in the future, you or a family member may be evaluated by a medical professional for possible cognitive impairment. Anyone with memory concerns needs an initial screening evaluation. You may be unaware that all Medicare beneficiaries can be screened as part of the annual wellness visit. This was initiated in 2011 as part of the Affordable Care Act. It includes a patient history, clinician observations, and concerns expressed by the patient or family.[6]

Simple assessment tools can detect possible dementia and determine if additional evaluations are needed. These screening tests may include the General Practitioner Assessment of Cognition exam, the "Mini-Cog" screening for Cognitive Impairment in Older Adults, a Memory Impairment Screen, an Informant Interview to Differentiate Aging and Dementia, or a Short Informant Questionnaire of Cognitive Decline in the Elderly.[7] These tools include most of the symptoms listed in the self-assessment in chapter 1 or in the mental exercises below.

Consider working with a partner and adding these mental exercises to your routine:

- *Verbal memory*—Give three (to ten) words to remember and ask to repeat now and again later.
- *Verbal fluency*—Give sixty seconds to name as many words as possible in a word category (e.g., foods, pets, recreation). Next, give sixty seconds to name as many words as possible that begin with a given letter.
- *Working memory*—Give random numbers of increasing size and ask to repeat the numbers from highest to lowest.
- *Motor speed*—Place one hundred small tokens (one at a time) into a container for sixty seconds as quickly as possible.
- *Information*—Tell something that happened in the news in the last week, with as many details as possible.
- *Emotional distractibility and memory*—Give twenty words: ten objects (e.g., ball, cracker) and ten with emotional value (e.g., romance, cancer). Ask to recall all the words, then recall the two lists separately.

These assessments may be given in a clinical setting:

- *Reasoning and problem solving*—Look at two pictures simultaneously; each picture shows three different colored balls arranged differently on three pegs. Determine the fewest number of times the balls in one picture would need to be moved to make the arrangement identical to the opposing picture.

- *Attention and processing speed*—Various timed matching and sorting exercises.

Choose Well

Give Your Brain a Change of Pace

Weekends are fun because of the change of pace. So are vacations and holidays. But to go a step further, it helps your mind when you mix up routines with different activities. Try some new things and break up your routines.

Choose brain-building activities that are reasonably complex, varied, new, and challenging and do them frequently. For instance, try some online brain fitness apps. They probably won't make you smarter or happier, but they may help you perform certain tasks better. You won't notice any drastic transformation, but it's worth a try. Any cognitively demanding tasks are a good change of pace for your brain. Here are some ideas:

Learn some conversational words in a foreign language.

Switch around your morning activities and try to do things with the opposite hand.

Trade seats around the dinner table; it changes conversations and the view of the room.

Open the car windows and notice the sounds and smells on your route.

Stay informed about what's going on in the world.

Read books and newspapers; join a book club.

Tutor reading or other areas of interest to the young or elderly or to people who use English as their second language.

Volunteer (social connections are good for your brain).

Do your own math; resist using a calculator.

Turn table-top pictures, clocks, or a calendar upside down.

At the grocery store, stop and look at the shelves, top to bottom. If there's something you've never seen before, read the ingredients and think about it. You don't have to buy it to benefit.

Visit cultural sites when you travel.

Visit area museums and historic sites in the county where you live.

Shop at new grocery stores and cook new recipes.

Try new hobbies.

Play "thinking" games such as Scrabble, cards, checkers, or chess.

The Magic of Prefixes, Suffixes, and Roots

Knowing common prefixes, suffixes, and root words and how to use them can unlock the meaning of thousands of words. Each prefix might hold the key to one hundred words.

For example, *mal* means "bad." Knowing this, you can guess the meaning of malabsorption, maladapted, maladjusted, maladministration, maladroit, malady, malaise, malapropos, malcontent, malediction, malefactor, malfeasance, malformation, malfunction, malignancy, malinger, malnourished, malpractice, and maltreatment.[8]

Brain Boosters

A person's vocabulary reflects his or her overall general knowledge. Words, knowledge, and memory are all related. You can learn many words from studying English, literature, art, music, biology, and history. That's one reason why the Brain Boosters are included at the end of every chapter.

Warm-Up Vocabulary Quiz

The brain can comprehend a one-word definition better than a long one, so the definitions are best kept short. It's usually not enough to just read through a list of new words with their definitions and try to remember them. Once you learn the correct definitions, review them over a period of two weeks to help store the words in your permanent memory. This also aids neuroplasticity.

Circle the correct definition for the words below. Research the correct answer if you are unsure, then say it aloud and use the word in a sentence.

1. abide
   A. to leave
   B. to love
   C. to remain/wait
   D. to persuade

2. bamboozle
   A. to prohibit
   B. to deceive
   C. to defer/delay
   D. to lull/soothe

3. caveat
   A. warning
   B. encouragement
   C. cave
   D. conclave

4. decry
   A. to welcome
   B. to detain
   C. to design
   D. to denounce

5. doff
   A. to take off/remove
   B. to put on
   C. to drink
   D. to dote/love

6. descry
   A. decry/denounce
   B. catch sight of something
   C. cry
   D. hopeless

7. catamaran
   A. cat
   B. dictator
   C. raft
   D. matron

8. proffer
   A. to rescind
   B. to poke
   C. to offer
   D. to play

9. trek
   A. to trick
   B. to trespass
   C. to travel
   D. to argue

10. wily
    A. weary/tired
    B. cunning/sly
    C. mean
    D. wild

Literary Classics

The classics have something for everyone, including culture, history, and philosophy. They are entertaining, enlightening, and challenging and encourage mental versatility.

Are all of the authors and their famous works correct?

750 BC	Homer, *The Iliad* (about the Trojan wars; Homer is considered to be the first writer of Western literature)
380 BC	Plato, *Republic* (first book of Western philosophy)
1478	Geoffrey Chaucer, *The Canterbury Tales* (brought literature to the middle class)
1605/1615	Cervantes Saavedra, *Don Quixote* in two volumes (the first modern novel)
1667	John Milton, *Paradise Lost*
1697	William Shakespeare, *Romeo and Juliet* (Shakespeare is the greatest English poet and dramatist)
1726	Jonathan Swift, *Gulliver's Travels*
1732	Benjamin Franklin, *Poor Richard's Almanac*
1813	Jane Austen, *Pride and Prejudice*
1818	Mary Shelley, *Frankenstein*
1845	Edgar Allan Poe, "The Crow"
1850	Nathaniel Hawthorne, *The Scarlet Letter*
1851	Herman Melville, *Moby-Dick*
1852	Harriet Beecher Stowe, *Uncle Tom's Cabin*
1854	Henry David Thoreau, *Walden*
1855	Walt Whitman, *Leaves of Grass* (first edition)
1860–61	Charles Dickens, *Great Expectations*
1866	Fyodor Dostoevsky, *Crime and Punishment*
1869	Leo Nikolayevich Tolstoy, *War and Peace*
1884	Mark Twain (Samuel Clemens), *Huckleberry Finn* (first edition)

1894	George Bernard Shaw, *Arms and the Man*
1906	Upton Sinclair, *The Jungle*
1916	Robert Frost, "The Road Not Taken"
1922	T. S. Eliot, "The Waste Land"
1926	Sinclair Lewis, *Elmer Gantry*
1929	William Faulkner, *The Sound and the Fury*
1929	Ernest Hemingway, *A Farewell to Arms*
1939	John Steinbeck, *Grapes of Wrath*
1944	Tennessee Williams, *The Glass Menagerie*
1949	Arthur Miller, *Death of a Salesman*
1973	Aleksandr Isayevich Solzhenitsyn, *The Gulag Archipelago*
1982	Alice Walker, *The Color Purple*
1997	J. K. Rowling, *Harry Potter and the Philosopher's Stone*

True (correct) _____   **False** (incorrect) _____

11

Broad Knowledge—Better Brain

IT'S A FACT: The brain is programmed with knowledge. The broader the knowledge, the better the brain thinks, remembers, and stays sharp for life satisfaction.

For many years, I answered call-in mental health questions on a national daily radio program. I responded to questions ranging from neurology to psychology, physiology, biochemistry, pharmacology, and theology. Callers sometimes asked me if I was using a computer to get detailed information so quickly. I answered, "Yes, I have the most matchless computer ever made—the human brain."

I've worked a lifetime to program a wide range of knowledge into my brain. Each area stimulates the other areas because of how the brain works. These educational efforts remind me of a sign I saw on a high school bulletin board in Dallas: "Free every Monday through Friday—knowledge. Bring your own containers."[1]

Other quips about knowledge have also caught my attention:[2]

I'm convinced that knowledge is power—to overcome the past, to change our own situations, to fight new obstacles, to make better decisions.

Ben Carson, *Think Big: Unleashing
Your Potential for Excellence*

In the age of information, ignorance is a choice.

Donny Miller, author

If you are not willing to learn, no one can help you. If you are determined to learn, no one can stop you.

Zig Ziglar, motivational speaker

Knowledge is power, and enthusiasm pulls the switch.

Steve Droke, author

An investment in knowledge always pays the best interest.

Benjamin Franklin, statesman and scientist

We See Broad Knowledge at Work Everywhere

The broader our knowledge, the better we do in every aspect of our lives—family, work, health, spirituality, relationships, recreation, finances, education, and community.

We can keep building general knowledge through reading, experiences, education, and even just observing others. It pays off in intelligence, confidence, and open-mindedness.

It even helps us make informed decisions, increases opportunities and influence on others, and gives us an edge in our careers.

Employers are focusing more on hiring people who have a broad range of knowledge and experience as well as field-specific skills. They value people who can bring more innovation, communication, and problem-solving skills, as well as a sense of social responsibility, because these are crucial to the success of companies in today's economy.

The important thing is to stay well-informed and keep learning. You never know when it will come in handy. Even if you find yourself in tough circumstances, such as losing a job or your health, you'll never lose your knowledge.

Keep Feeding Your Brain

We eat three times a day to feed our bodies, so shouldn't we regularly feed information to our brains? This needs to be an ongoing process, not just random encounters. It's not enough to read something once and hope it sticks. This "feeding" can be fun because there is always something new to learn in your areas of interest. Read special-interest magazines and books. Surf favorite topics on the internet. The average person browses through about one hundred internet domains each month, according to a Nielsen estimate in 2013. But that's just a small start. There are about one billion sites on the internet, which provide a lot of food for thought.[3]

Trying to summarize the different types of knowledge is difficult because there's no master list. There are many opinions on knowledge categories, but for my purpose, I'll use these three: personal, procedural, and propositional.

Personal knowledge is by acquaintance, the kind we have when we say things like "I know my spouse."

Procedural knowledge is how to do something such as juggle or drive. It's having the knowledge to perform skills.

Propositional knowledge is having facts. When we say things such as "I know that the three angles of a triangle add up to 180 degrees" or "I know you ate my pickle," we have propositional knowledge.

It's the propositional knowledge—the facts—that can build our intellect and improve our memory. Try to put a plan like the following into action:

- Make a list of your special interests and decide where you'll find new information about them. For instance, do you want to know more about crafting gifts, car repair, medical conditions, fitness, travel, entertainment, or fishing?
- Learn about and keep reviewing the new information in these areas to revitalize your brain circuits.
- Also study and review broad knowledge topics such as cultural literacy. The one hundred general knowledge facts at the end of this chapter (see Brain Boosters) are designed to stimulate your brain. Once you find all the right answers, review them over and over.

- Keep learning new words and their meanings (see appendix C).
- Push your brain to reason better and to improve rapid processing of information. There are online exercises and memory games for that too.

Your job is to keep feeding knowledge to your brain. The goal is to keep the neurotransmitters, synaptic connections, and nerve impulses along the pathways of brain circuits, chemicals, and neurons all working together in a constant, smooth, organized process. Balance and harmony of the parts that store and process your memory are the goal.

To put it a simpler way, for neurons to become active, they must receive stimuli. Each neuron has many dendrites that receive electrical messages, and the dendritic fields can be increased through *personal education*. Keep your dendrites fired up!

The Harmony of Broad Knowledge and Memory

Universities of liberal arts have long recognized that intelligence partially revolves around a diverse education; I would add that cognition and memory do also. *Remember*: Studying a broad range of topics causes neuroplasticity and neurogenesis, and increases cognition with improved memory. This is important if you're interested in keeping your brain sharp and reducing your risk of mental decline.

When asked to explain what memory is, many people would say, "It's everything I know and all the important times of my life that I remember." But it's much more than that.

We're typically not aware of what's in our memory until we need to use that information. Much of the recall process happens without even having to concentrate on it, particularly with common tasks such as tying shoes and writing. But there are other types of memories that take more effort to conjure up when we need them.

Memories are stored in words, concepts, images, sounds, touch, and even the sense of smell. They can be long lasting and vivid, but they can also be susceptible to partial forgetting and inaccuracies. They continually change and are revised because of retrieval and recollection issues.

There are different types of memory, and we use all of them. Each type has a specific purpose and is stored for different lengths in our memory, but they all work together.

- *Sensory memory* is the shortest-term element of memory (as little as one second). It retains quick sight, hearing, smell, taste, and touch information. It's what keeps you from running into the person walking toward you and what allows you to line up a button and buttonhole on your pants without looking.

- *Short-term memory* is our primary, working memory. These memories are around up to only a few days, and even less unless they get "attention." A small amount of information is held in an active, readily available state for this brief time. People who suffer from short-term memory loss may not remember what they ate for breakfast but can remember childhood friends. Alzheimer's disease and dementias can cause some attention impairment. Also, sleep deprivation, pain, psychoactive drugs, and many other things can interfere with attention and reduce one's ability to recall things we would expect to be in short-term memory.

- *Long-term memory* has an unlimited capacity for retention, retrieval, and recognition over a lifetime. Information about things you are interested in is likely to be stored here. (It is supported by other types of memory, including explicit, unconscious, declarative, procedural, episodic, and semantic memories.)

Some of you may be starting to realize that your memory capacity is weakening due to age or medical reasons. But you can do something about it, and the sooner, the better. Try to avoid sitting in front of a television all day. Get up and take short walks. Get a change of scenery every day. Pick up things to read and participate in conversations. You'll regret it if you wait too long.

Also remember that knowledge not reviewed will fade, so review what you learn. It's the key to securing it in your long-term memory. By reviewing an area of interest or a little broad knowledge each day and by pushing your brain to remember details faster, the brain circuitry is revitalized, and connections and cells are increased.

I'm keeping this chapter short because I want you to use your time and energy to review the one hundred general knowledge facts in the following Brain Boosters section. No one is too young or too old to work through this general knowledge exercise. Don't skip it—for your brain's sake. Once you figure out all the correct answers, come back and review them often. The more you review the information, the faster your reviews will go. Soon you'll be working these facts into your conversations and impressing your family and friends.

Choose Well

The ability to interpret proverbs, work with conceptual problems, and solve puzzles involves abstract thinking. Interpreting proverbs and idioms can boost your abstract thinking (using concepts and making and understanding generalizations). The interpretation is given for the following proverbs:

> Knowledge is power.
> > Sir Francis Bacon,
> > *Religious Meditations*
>
> *The more one knows, the more one will be able to control events and reactions to events.*
>
> Genius is 1 percent inspiration and 99 percent perspiration.
> > Thomas Edison, inventor and businessman
>
> *Great accomplishments depend not so much on ingenuity but far more on hard work.*
>
> Slow but steady wins the race.
> > Aesop's fable,
> > *The Tortoise and the Hare*
>
> *Consistent, effective effort leads to success.*

You can lead a horse to water, but you can't make him drink.

1175 adage

You can show people the way to do things, but you can't force them to act.

Don't cross a bridge before you get to it.

proverb

Don't worry over anticipated difficulties in life.

Don't count your chickens before they hatch.

Samuel Butler, poet

Don't consider the surety of an event before it happens.

He who lives in a glass house shouldn't throw stones.

Geoffrey Chaucer, author

We all have faults, so we shouldn't be overly critical of others.

The apple falls not far from the tree.

idiom

Children are like their parents.

Idioms are expressions that make no sense if translated literally. Can you interpret the following idioms and use each one in a sentence?

flash in the pan	eat crow
on the warpath	wet blanket
cold feet	green thumb
sitting duck	tip of the iceberg

hold water

throw the book at someone

know the ropes

split hairs

lion's share

shot in the dark

play possum

run of the mill

tongue-in-cheek

glad-hander

wet behind the ears

under the wire

Brain Boosters

Learning can be tiring, so stay conservative in the amount you attempt—start simple. For example, review one paragraph in a previous area of expertise per day, one informational entry in this book per day, one fact in cultural literacy per day, and one new vocabulary word per day (see appendix C).

You can progress in steady, small amounts. The important thing is to stay persistent. Increase the amount as appropriate. Eventually learning in patterns of seven is ideal—seven paragraphs of area of expertise, seven facts of cultural literacy, seven new vocabulary words—and work on shortening the time it takes you.

What Do You Know?

Test your knowledge as well as rekindle old memory tracks with the following one hundred general knowledge facts. If you don't know the answers, please research the information online instead of just guessing. The information will last longer in your memory when you look up answers on your own. Once you've determined and recorded all the correct answers, review them often for several months to commit the knowledge into your long-term memory.

General Knowledge Facts

	True	False
1. Robert Frost, the most popular twentieth-century American poet, wrote "The Road Not Taken" and "Stopping by Woods on a Snowy Evening."	_____	_____
2. Are the following definitions correct?	_____	_____

    a. biology—the study of living things

    b. physics—the study of the interaction of matter and energy

    c. chemistry—the study of elements, compounds, and their reactions

    d. English—the study of the parts of speech

    e. geology—the study of the earth

	True	False
3. Hydrogen has an atomic number of 1.	_____	_____
4. A laser is a beam of light.	_____	_____
5. Are the following associations correct?	_____	_____

United States of America	Washington, DC
Mexico	Mexico City
Russia	Moscow
Switzerland	Bern
United Kingdom	London
Spain	Madrid
Iran	Tehran
Iraq	Baghdad
Japan	Tokyo
Australia	Canberra
Egypt	Cairo
Bahamas	Nassau

	True	False

6. Currencies vary with the country. Are the following associations correct?

USA	dollar	South Africa	rand
Russia	ruble	Ghana (Gold Coast)	cedi
Switzerland	franc	Iraq	dinar
Mexico	peso	China	yuan
Saudi Arabia	riyal	Japan	yen
United Kingdom	pound	Sweden	krona
Israel	shekel		

7. The Alps are in Switzerland, and the Himalayas are in Nepal.

8. The abbreviation for "for example" is e.g., and the abbreviation for "namely" is viz.

9. AM is amplitude modulation in radio signals; FM is frequency modulation.

10. Sandra Day O'Connor was the first female Supreme Court justice; Sally Ride was America's first female astronaut.

11. The largest countries by land size in order are:
    1. Russia
    2. Canada
    3. United States of America
    4. China
    5. Brazil
    6. Australia
    7. India
    8. Argentina
    9. Kazakhstan
    10. Algeria

12. The largest continents in order are:
    1. Asia
    2. Africa
    3. North America
    4. South America
    5. Europe

	True	False

    6. Antarctica

    7. Australia

13. The largest oceans in order are:

    1. Pacific

    2. Atlantic

    3. Indian

    4. Antarctic

    5. Arctic

14. Farming villages around the Mediterranean Gulf appeared around 10,000 BC.

15. Geometry started around 1000 BC.

16. The Olympic Games started in 776 BC.

17. Leif Erikson reached North America around 1000 AD.

18. Marco Polo traveled to China in 1271.

19. Bartolomeu Dias sailed around the southern tip of Africa (the Cape of Good Hope) in 1488.

20. Christopher Columbus discovered America in 1492.

21. Vasco Nuñez de Balboa saw the Pacific Ocean in 1513.

22. Ferdinand Magellan sailed around the world in 1519–22.

23. The Great Lakes are:

    H—Huron

    O—Ontario

    M—Michigan

    E—Erie

    S—Superior

24. The average person in the United States watches television more than five hours per day.

25. Madison Avenue's business and economics district made New York City popular.

	True	False
26. The sculptures of four US presidents on Mount Rushmore include Washington, Jefferson, Lincoln, and Theodore Roosevelt.	___	___
27. The first permanent English settlement in North America was Jamestown, Virginia, in 1607.	___	___
28. The US military academy, West Point, is located in New York State.	___	___
29. The smallest continent is Australia.	___	___
30. The Black Sea is located between two continents, Europe and Asia.	___	___
31. The countries of Central America are Belize, Costa Rica, El Salvador, Guatemala, Honduras, Nicaragua, and Panama.	___	___
32. The country with the largest population is China.	___	___
33. The lowest point on earth is the Dead Sea at approximately 1,385 feet below sea level.	___	___
34. The capital of Scotland is Edinburgh.	___	___
35. Greenland is part of Denmark.	___	___
36. The former name of Iran is Persia.	___	___
37. Latitude refers to the north and south directions off the equator.	___	___
38. One of the smallest countries in the world is Liechtenstein (62 square miles) in the Alps between Austria and Switzerland.	___	___
39. The highest mountain in the world is Mount Everest.	___	___
40. There are seven continents on planet Earth surrounded by five oceans.	___	___
41. The largest and deepest ocean basin is the Pacific Ocean.	___	___
42. The city of Austin is the capital of Texas.	___	___
43. The capital of Cuba is Havana.	___	___

	True	False
44. An archipelago is a chain of islands.	_____	_____
45. A lagoon is a shallow body of water between a reef and the shore.	_____	_____
46. The largest freshwater lake in the world is Lake Superior. It is bordered by Ontario, Minnesota, Wisconsin, and Michigan.	_____	_____
47. The Nile River is the longest river in the world at 4,160 miles.	_____	_____
48. The highest waterfall in the world (979 meters) is Angel Falls in Venezuela.	_____	_____
49. Epistemology is the study of knowledge and justified belief.	_____	_____
50. Ghana was formerly called the Gold Coast.	_____	_____
51. Hawaii was formerly known as the Sandwich Islands.	_____	_____
52. Cuba's currency is the peso.	_____	_____
53. In ancient math, the Roman numeral "X" means "10."	_____	_____
54. Aristotle developed the theory of causality: the relation between an event, the *cause*, and a second event, the *effect*, where the second event is understood as a consequence of the first.	_____	_____
55. In chemistry, Na stands for sodium in the periodic table.	_____	_____
56. Tulips and baby's breath are examples of perennial plants (live more than two years).	_____	_____
57. CO_2 is the chemical symbol for carbon dioxide, a colorless, odorless gas.	_____	_____
58. Steel products can be recycled repeatedly without loss of strength.	_____	_____
59. A Geiger counter measures radioactive emissions.	_____	_____

	True	False

60. Birthstone (gemstone) colors vary by the month. Are the following associations correct? ___ ___

January	garnet (dark red by variable)
February	amethyst (purple)
March	aquamarine (light blue-green), bloodstone (dark green/red spots)
April	diamond
May	emerald (green)
June	alexandrite, pearl, moonstone (green)
July	ruby (red)
August	peridot (light green), sardonyx (green)
September	sapphire (blue)
October	opal (white), tourmaline (iridescent display of colors)
November	citrine (yellow to brown), topaz
December	turquoise, zircon (greenish blue), tanzanite, light blue topaz

61. Longitude is the geographic angular distance east or west of the prime meridian. ___ ___

62. Humans belong to the Homo sapiens species; the class is known as Mammalia. ___ ___

63. A prime number is any number greater than one that can only be factored by itself and the number one. ___ ___

64. One year has 52 weeks or 8,760 hours. ___ ___

65. Most years have 365 days or 525,600 minutes. ___ ___

66. One mile equals 5,280 feet or 1,760 yards. ___ ___

67. One kilogram equals 1,000 grams or 2.2046 pounds. ___ ___

68. Isaac Newton was the "father of the study of physics." ___ ___

69. The chemistry pH scale ranges from 0 to 14 and measures how acidic or basic (alkaline) a substance is. A pH of 7 is neutral. A pH less than 7 is acidic. A pH greater than 7 is basic. ___ ___

	True	False

70. According to Fahrenheit the freezing temperature of water is 32 degrees and the boiling point is 212 degrees.

71. $18 \div 2 = 9$ and $9 \times 2 = 18$.

72. Any number multiplied by zero equals zero.

73. Not all brain cells are alike. There are as many as ten thousand specific types of neurons in the brain.

74. One kilometer equals 0.62 miles.

75. France is divided into departments, Canada into provinces, and the USA into states.

76. There are 206 bones in the adult human body, 46 chromosomes, and 32 teeth.

77. The 1813 Louisiana Purchase was the acquisition by the United States of France's claim to the Louisiana Territory.

78. Alaska was purchased in 1867 by the United States.

79. Anniversary gifts vary by the year. Are the following associations correct (traditional/modern)?

    1 paper/clocks
    2 cotton/china
    3 leather/crystal or glass
    4 fruit or flowers/appliances
    5 wood/silverware
    6 candy or iron/wood
    7 wool or copper/desk sets
    8 pottery or bronze/linens or lace

    9 pottery/leather
    10 tin or aluminum/diamond jewelry
    15 crystal/watches
    20 china/platinum
    30 pearl/diamond
    40 ruby/ruby
    50 gold/gold
    60 diamond/diamond

80. The skin is the largest organ in the body; the femur is the longest bone.

	True	False
81. Are the following measurement associations correct?	___	___

photometer	light
barometer	atmospheric pressure
audiometer	sound
galvanometer	electrical connection
anemometer	wind speed
bolometer	radiant energy/radiation
densitometer film	darkness of photographic or semitransparent material
calorie	energy heat
sphygmomanometer	blood pressure
manometer	pressure

82. The largest seas include the Coral, Arabian, Mediterranean, and Bering.   ___ ___

83. In poetry a sonnet is fourteen lines and a haiku is three lines.   ___ ___

84. In baseball there are nine players, in basketball there are five players, and in football there are eleven players.   ___ ___

85. Award cups in sports include the World Cup in soccer, the Stanley Cup in hockey, and the America's Cup in yachting.   ___ ___

86. The human body temperature is 98.6 degrees F (Fahrenheit) or 37 degrees C (Celsius).   ___ ___

87. The White House is located at 1600 Pennsylvania Avenue; the British prime minister lives at 10 Downing Street.   ___ ___

88. Various organisms can invade the body. Are the following associations correct?   ___ ___

amoebic dysentery	protozoan parasite
chicken pox	virus
Rocky Mountain Spotted Fever	rickettsia bacteria
strep throat	bacteria

	True	False

89. Learning new things produces physical changes in the brain structure. These changes can be seen on MRI scans. ___ ___

90. The capacity of short-term memory is limited to about seven items for twenty to thirty seconds. It can be stretched by using memory strategies such as chunking. ___ ___

91. The largest desert is the Sahara (3.5 million square miles) in northern Africa. ___ ___

92. In the grading of meat, "prime" is the best; "choice" is next. ___ ___

93. Myopia is nearsightedness; hyperopia is farsightedness. ___ ___

94. On a ship, the front is the bow, the rear is the stern, the right side is starboard, and the left side is port. ___ ___

95. Are the following sports categories correct? ___ ___

bat-and-ball games	baseball, cricket
racquet-and-ball games	tennis, squash, racquetball
hand-and-ball-striking games	handball, 4 square
goal games	basketball, football, hockey, lacrosse
net games	volleyball
target games	bowling, lot ball

96. Richter measures the magnitude of earthquakes; Mohs measures the hardness of solid objects. ___ ___

97. Are the following associations correct? ___ ___

Land of the Rising Sun	Japan
Seine River	France
Thames River	England
Andes	South America
Alps	Europe

	True	False

98. The lowest ranked officer in the army is a second lieutenant, whereas the lowest in the navy is an ensign. A general wears stars, a colonel wears an eagle, a major wears an oak leaf, and a sergeant wears stripes.

99. Are the following associations correct?

Chicago	Midway
Boston	Logan
Washington	Dulles
Hartford	Bradley
Las Vegas	McCarran

100. Are the following numbers correct?

Seven months have thirty-one days; four months have thirty days (April, June, September, and November). February has twenty-eight days except every fourth/ leap year.

12

Finish Well!

IT'S A FACT: You know what is good for your brain. Make wise choices today so you can feel better, think better, and live better tomorrow. The good thing about your brain is that the more you use it, the better it gets.

In April 2016, Patti Davis Reagan, author, actress, and daughter of President Ronald Reagan and Nancy Reagan, wrote the following testimony about her father's battle with Alzheimer's disease:

Alzheimer's doesn't care if you are President of the United States or a dockworker. It steals what is most precious to a human being—memories, connections, the familiar landmarks of a lifetime that we all come to rely on to hold our place secure in this world and keep us linked to those we have come to know and love. I watched as fear invaded my father's eyes—this man who was never afraid of anything. I heard his voice tremble as he stood in the living room and said, "I don't know where I am." I watched helplessly as he reached for memories, for words, that were suddenly out of reach and moving farther away. For ten long years he drifted—past the memories that marked his life, past all that was familiar . . . and mercifully, finally past the fear.

Alzheimer's is the ultimate pirate, pillaging a person's life and leaving an empty landscape behind. It sweeps up entire families, forcing everyone to claw their way through overwhelming grief, confusion, helplessness, and anger. . . .

Twice a week I run a support group called Beyond Alzheimer's for caregivers and family members of those with Alzheimer's and dementia. I look into haunted eyes that remind me of my own when my father was ill. I listen to stories of helplessness and loss and am continually moved by the bravery of those who wake up every morning not knowing who their loved one will be that day, or what will be lost. The only certainty with Alzheimer's is that more will be lost and the disease will always win in the end.[1]

Don't Add to These Statistics

About one in nine families will experience the anguish of Alzheimer's, a disease that has no cure. One in four adults suffers from a diagnosable mental disorder. One in ten has a drug problem. One in five children under eighteen has a diagnosable mental disorder. Many people and their families are obviously hurting.[2]

I'm concerned about all of these people as well as all who have yet to observe mental decline firsthand. The threat of age-related memory impairment looms over everyone, and the importance of preventive care still eludes our society as a whole. The general public expects there will be a quick fix if it ever happens to them. They assume doctors will simply prescribe pills to clear up their brain fog.

Note: Most people over age sixty-five take an average of seven medications regularly. The aging body absorbs, metabolizes, distributes, and excretes drugs much differently than that of a young person. As all these chemicals and stresses interact, and as medical problems increase, the mind and body get out of sync. We are all physical, emotional, social, psychological, and spiritual beings, and everything that happens to us affects each of these dimensions; they're all interrelated. When one area is stressed or damaged, it can knock our whole life off balance.

The "Law" of Personal Well-Being Is *No Pain, No Gain*

No two people age exactly the same way or at the same rate. One person can seem elderly at age fifty; another can seem young at age seventy. Each birthday turns into an opportunity to appraise our physical, mental, social, and financial conditions.

When you look in the mirror, do you see someone so smart and secure that you don't need to prepare your brain for the long haul? Take another look. You have 24 hours each day to use any way you want. That's 168 hours a week; 8,760 hours a year. Certainly you can find a few moments to invest in your long-term quality of life.

A healthy lifestyle and common sense are the keys, and they're in your control. Instead of making the usual list of New Year's resolutions, make a commitment to stay aware of how your lifestyle choices are affecting your brain. So many people start with good intentions, but how many people sustain them? Don't cop out by thinking, "I'll deal with it when I get a little older." Don't settle for just drifting into old age and watching your mind and body fade away. In the case of mental decline, a little fear can be a good motivator.

Decide on Your Personal Brain-Care Action Plan

The good news is that your mental health responds to nurturing. This book has given you some facts about your amazing brain as well as some sobering warnings about aging. Embracing the practical insights and advice may keep you from becoming another dementia statistic. Refer to this book often to review the how-to tips, action lists, self-assessments, and quizzes. That will keep you on track.

If you have highlighted some of the recommendations, you already have a good start for making your own plan for brain care. You are solely responsible for deciding on the content and extent of your plan and for following it. When you find yourself slacking on regular mental exercise, refresh your action plan to keep it interesting. Commit to staying motivated to protect your mental health so the people and things you care about don't drift away.

Make a list of things you can do to exercise your brain and post it on the refrigerator. For the activities that may take a little time, decide how much time a week you can spend on them. Be realistic and flexible. It's keeping up with the short-term goals that will get you to long-term success.

Here are a few basics that can help you get started:

- Make daily behavioral changes. Eat breakfast, read a short devotional message, choose three things you want to accomplish each day, include a social contact, get fresh air, and so on.
- Get regular medical checkups and comply with treatment plans. (Your physical health impacts your mental health.)
- Keep changing up your routines a little bit. It's good for your brain.
- Enlist others to help you stay on track (accountability buddies).
- Embrace health trends. Better nutrition and more physical and mental exercise will clear your head and invigorate you.
- Identify and reduce your bad habits. The damage may be reversible.
- Laugh more. Check out funny books and movies from the library.
- Go somewhere every day, and read everything you can get your hands on—food labels at the grocery store, church bulletins, or even junk mail.
- Make sure your daily lifestyle choices reflect your core values and goals.

Make Memories Part of Your Brain-Care Action Plan

It's a good idea to make a list of your special memories and add to it as often as you can. We know from personal experience that it's not always the big events that make a permanent impression on our minds. Sometimes it's the small, daily incidences that remain in our minds for a lifetime. If these are recorded, the fantasy and reality can be sorted out as memories grow old. Having journals with treasured memories will be a future blessing to you as well as a helpful aid to your caregivers.

Start gathering some of the following keepsakes and write down memories of the topics below. Adding more details in the coming years will be a blessing to you and your family.

- photo albums and scrapbooks
- notebook to jot down family memories such as:
  milestones
  holiday traditions
  favorite friends
  interesting facts about ancestors
  homes and cars
  family jokes and sayings
  honors, achievements
  pets
  childhood
  vacations
  schools and churches
  "firsts"
  happiness is . . .
  fears and mistakes
  the little things
  hopes
  sports
  favorite foods

Choose to Do Something Different Tomorrow

I've treated many people over the years who were experiencing early mental decline because of prolonged substance abuse and other unhealthy lifestyle choices. It was especially concerning when they were only in their twenties, thirties, and forties because they were putting their brains at risk for long-term damage.

If you can relate to the following situations or other examples in this book, please recognize the urgency of choosing to do some things differently. Sometimes simple lifestyle adjustments and common sense can get your brain health back in balance.

Steve, a single thirty-eight-year-old information technology programmer, has always worked from home. Lately, he feels like he's working in slow motion. He has to double-check his work because he sometimes misses steps, so he's working longer hours to meet his deadlines. He is visibly distraught over the fear that he is losing his cognition. He's tried doing crossword puzzles but hasn't noticed any improvement in his brain fog. Steve needs socializing and more stimulating mental and physical activities to reboot his brain health. He's going to try something different tomorrow.

Emily is a forty-one-year-old secretary in a nearby office building. She came to see me because she feels overwhelmed and stressed, and has trouble concentrating at work. She can't adjust to the new computer systems and feels her memory is slipping. She spends her evenings watching TV from bed because she's too tired to do anything else. I suggested she try something different in her routine, so she started going to a gym several times a week, goes for walks with coworkers during her lunch hour, and has borrowed some popular books. These changes are helping her manage the workplace stress because she feels more alert and confident.

You. "I'm _____ years old and spend the majority of my time _____. I've followed the same routines for about _____ years and consider my lifestyle to be _____. After working through the self-assessments and checklists in this book, I'm aware that I need to _____. I'm motivated to keep my brain fit and have circled thirty brain-care tips that I can start right away. I'm choosing to do some things differently from now on."

Happiness Is Your Choice

I'm thinking of the children's song, "If you're happy and you know it, clap your hands . . . then your face will surely show it." My bestselling book is *Happiness Is a Choice*. Everybody wants to feel happy, and mental fitness plays an important role.

Happiness is more than a passing mood. It's about making the most of good times and bad times and experiencing the best possible life overall. It helps us achieve personal ambitions and even live longer. We feel healthier both physically and emotionally and are more energetic, compassionate, creative, and fun to be around. Likely, our happiness makes our friends, families, and colleagues feel happier too.

Some people choose happiness but still don't obtain it because they seek inner peace and joy in the wrong places such as materialism or powerful positions. Choose healthy attitudes, behaviors, and mental fitness. Your brain can help you do this.

Tap Into Your "Happy" Neurotransmitters

You feel good when your brain releases dopamine, serotonin, endorphins, or oxytocin. These neurotransmitters aren't "on" all the time but you can get them to kick in. When you understand what they do, your ups and downs make sense.[3]

Dopamine motivates you to meet goals, desires, and needs, and gives you a surge of pleasure when achieving them. This causes neurons to connect and wires your brain to expect a reward in similar situations. Instead of celebrating only when you meet a goal, set little milestones to release dopamine more often. These connections trigger a good feeling with each step and inspire you to finish. If you're a team leader or employer, recognize the accomplishments of your team with gift cards or food. This gives them a dopamine hit and inspires future motivation and productivity. Other examples: marijuana releases dopamine but gets people addicted to the "high" feeling. When people talk about themselves, their brains release dopamine so they want to keep doing it. Procrastination, self-doubt, and lack of enthusiasm are linked with low levels of dopamine.

Confidence triggers *serotonin*. It kicks in when you feel important or significant and is absent when you feel lonely or depressed. Getting reminders that you're valued gives you a serotonin boost. So if you're having a bad day, remember past achievements and happy times. Another way to boost serotonin levels is to take a break outside and get direct sun for twenty minutes. Your skin absorbs ultraviolet rays that help produce vitamin D and serotonin. Too much UV light isn't good, but some daily exposure is healthy. Other ways to boost serotonin are showing gratitude to the people around you, eating bananas, and getting good sleep.

Endorphins are released to mask pain and stress due to physical activities and in emergencies. The runner's high only happens if you run to the point of pain; the euphoric surge is like getting a second wind. Endorphins also help alleviate anxiety and depression. The good news for most of us is that small releases are stimulated by laughter and exercise. Try watching a comedy video while on a treadmill and see how you feel. Scented oils (vanilla and lavender) and dark chocolate can also give you a boost.

The release of *oxytocin* is a little different. It creates a feeling of social trust and intimacy, and strengthens relationships. It's known as the "love hormone" because it binds healthy relationships. When a mother breast-feeds her baby, both mother and child release oxytocin, which leads to bonding. Giving someone a hug or a gift not only strengthens personal relationships but also raises your level of oxytocin.

Finishing Well

We quickly tire of new resolutions. We get bored and lazy and expect instant gratification. This book will probably get buried under a stack of magazines. Taking a few days off from your new "brain-care action plan" can turn into weeks and months of no effort. You know how it is. Making a commitment to keep your mind sharp is like running a marathon.

Starting is easy, but finishing is hard. Often, it's the lack of direction and commitment, not the lack of time, that's the problem.

Don't join the ranks of quitters. It's not okay to quit. Charles Swindoll described it well by saying we're nearing the "I'm-getting-tired-so-I'll-just-quit" mentality. Dieting is a discipline, so we stay fat. Finishing school is a hassle, so we bail out. Cultivating a close relationship is difficult, so we back off. Working through conflicts in a marriage is a tiring struggle, so we walk away. Sticking with an occupation is tough, so we start looking elsewhere.[4] Mental exercises seem repetitive or hard, so we figure we've done enough.

It takes self-discipline to maintain an improvement plan. Many of you will muster up the determination to begin. After the novelty fades, procrastination sets in. But hang tough. Do the necessary brain-boosting exercises, and keep the end in mind. Fight against mental decline.

Care. Before you no longer can care. Since memory is the guardian of so much, do it for yourself and your family. The motivation is there. You and your loved ones will benefit. The stakes are high.

It seems we hear the term "finishing well" mostly when someone finishes a race, retires, or passes away. It implies they've worked hard on something to the end. Motivation can get you started, and good habits will get you there. Investing effort in memory care is a lifelong investment.

Just Keep Going

Just keep going
when the lightning flashes and the thunder rolls,
when truculent torrents rage,
when storms circle.

Just keep going
when friends depart and difficulties mount,
when finances flee,
when the job demeans.

Just keep going
when health wobbles,
when changes war,
when relationships ramble.

Just keep going
with kind tones spoken,
with a redolent aroma emitted,
with a formidable mandate given.

Just keep going
with echoes of love from a few friends over the
    years,
with redoubtable messages over the years,
with the legacy of saints past.

Just keep going.
You can endure.
You can succeed.
You can. Just keep going.

Dr. Frank Minirth

Choose Well

Memories Are Fascinating

I have memories of skipping rocks on a creek in Arkansas, hiking the Appalachian Trail, and sitting in an old rocker on a porch under the shade trees. These series of little motion pictures from our past build on each other to set up our present and future attitudes and behaviors. They're tucked away in almost all parts of the human brain.

There are memories of everything that has happened to us—what we've read, television we've watched, people we've met—somewhere in our minds. We tend to remember simple messages that are profound or things that were repeated, as during learning. Our minds selectively pick out those memories that are applicable or personal, and we attach emotions to each of them. For instance, I feel calm when I go into a small church because I attended a small church when I was growing up. Memories also affect our attitudes and behaviors. There are certain people that I instantly like. For example, I like elderly people because I had some godly elderly people in my life as a child.

It's interesting how three or four children in the same family can have totally different memories of their parents and childhoods. Individual memory selection systems and perceptions are unique and personal. I recall going horseback riding with my dad as a young child, and I remember my mother rubbing my head. The emotions associated with these memories are wonderful. Riding with Dad was exciting and fun. With my mother, I felt secure and loved.

Memories Matter

Memories matter because they

give our lives meaning
help us cope with setbacks and grief
enrich our relationships
are reminders of blessings, loved ones, and milestones
cost nothing, yet the results are priceless

I'm thankful for my memories, which are locked away in my head like a private diary. I never want to lose any of them, so I fight daily to keep my memory strong and my mind sharp. I encourage you to do the same. Protect your memories by following the brain-care strategies in this book, and keep making deposits into the memory banks of your family members. These investments will become your legacy.

Conclusion

Have you ever noticed that every movie, book, sermon, or presentation gets summarized in one sentence for promotional purposes? The summary of this book might simply be, "Reduce your risk of mental decline." It's an action statement about making personal choices that can protect your memory and give you a better chance of making it through old age with your mind intact.

The insights and practical advice in this book are meant to be informative, supportive, and encouraging. I hope you will find them useful. Regardless of any poor choices you've made in the past, you can make better choices today. I've shared some of my personal stories, strengths, weaknesses, and most of all, my choices. Your choices matter too.

My hope is for each person to lead a healthy and happy life to the end. I want you to be gentle and patient with yourself and to relax in peace at the end of each day. As your life is enriched by God's love and grace, you, in turn, will be able to enrich the lives of those around you. Look at each day as an opportunity to make good choices for your spiritual, physical, emotional, and mental health.

God bless you on your personal journey.

Acknowledgments

I wish to thank the legions of people who have helped me through years of physical, psychological, professional, and spiritual growth. Included are theologians, medical doctors, authors, professors, friends, family, and, most of all, my loving wife, Mary Alice.

Special thanks to Jane Mack, science journalist, for preparing this manuscript for publication.

Appendix A

The Brain and Memory

Note: The following content may be technically difficult, but readers will glean a greater awareness of and appreciation for the complexity, vulnerabilities, and miraculous powers of the human brain.

It is not intended as a specific guide for any medical diagnosis or treatment; medical doctors should be consulted for all medical conditions. It includes general reference to common information. When deciding on specifics of any actions, symptoms, diagnoses, prognoses, or treatments, many aspects must be considered. The information given here may not be absolute or complete; variations, coinciding factors, pathologies, and updates might exist.[1]

aging with a healthy brain
- probable combination of genetic factors plus epigenetic factors allows some people to have well-functioning brains through old age

- genetic factors are multiple and include a lack of an APOE defect on chromosome 19
- epigenetic factors are also multiple and include a thick anterior cingulate area (probable genetic + epigenetic), physical and mental exercise, healthy diet, natural supplements, coping well with stress

anatomy of memory—overview

There are many types of memories in various regions of the brain. Knowledge of the neurological substrates is limited, and knowledge of how the many categories relate is also limited. Some brain areas are more important than others in memory, particularly the dorsolateral prefrontal cortex and the hippocampus.

- cerebrum
    lobes of the cerebral cortex
        frontal—memory, vocabulary, reason, personality, intellect, motor control, phonological loop (new vocabulary), birth to new memories (explicit memory)
        parietal—phonological loop (new vocabulary starts here), speech, sensory, involved in attention
        temporal—auditory and visual memory, parahippocampal gyrus
        occipital—visual information (insula—memory, integration)
    corpus collusum—connects hemispheres
    limbic system

    hippocampus—gives birth to new memories
        along with frontal lobes; explicit memory
        (facts and events)

    parahippocampal gyrus

    amygdala and intrusion—emotional memories

    nucleus accumbens and cingulate gyrus

  basal ganglia

- diencephalon

    thalamus and the internal capsule to cerebral
        cortex—relay center of sensory input except
        smell; the anterior plays a role in memory

    hypothalamus—visceral activities; fight or flight;
        signals pituitary gland that signals endocrine
        gland for physiological responses

    pituitary gland—endocrine functions

    pineal gland—melatonin

- brain stem

    midbrain—visual, auditory, and coordinating
        reflexes; contains the nuclei that produce
        neurotransmitters—serotonin, norepinephrine,
        and dopamine pons; relay center, respiratory
        rate

    medulla oblongata—relays sensory input and
        motor output

    cerebellum—involuntary coordination of skeletal
        muscles; implicit memory—retains past but
        does not recall it

- other brain areas of memory

precuneus—back center of brain; earliest retrieval; activation or shutdown of frontal cortex

nucleus basalis of Meynert—decline in this area correlates with Alzheimer's dementia and early cognitive delay; located in the basal forebrain; site of cholinergic cell bodies; axons project to hippocampus, amygdala, and neocortex; beta-amyloid and protein deposits theory; APOE protein theory

BDNF (brain-derived neurotrophic factor)

- a protein encoded by the BDNF gene
- increased in synaptic development and neural transmissions
- increased in plasticity and survival in multiple neurotransmitter systems

brain

- human brain (approximately three pounds) is a portion of the central nervous system; the receiver, organizer, and distributor of information for the body
- brain parts—the cerebrum with the cerebral cortex, limbic system, and basal ganglia; the diencephalon with the thalamus, hypothalamus, pituitary gland, and pineal gland; the midbrain; the pons and medulla; and the cerebellum
- number of cell types exceeds the number of all cell types in all other organs combined

- gray matter consists of nerve cell bodies and fibers; the white matter consists of myelinated nerve fibers and tracts

brain areas—overview of some functions

- cerebrum

  cerebral hemispheres are each divided into four lobes:

  frontal lobe—responsible for muscle movement, memory, and personality

  parietal lobe (sensory)—controls somatosensory issues such as touch, pain, pressure, and heat

  temporal lobe (sensory and auditory)—regulates sensory information integration and some auditory information integration

  occipital lobe (visual)—processes and relays visual information

  cerebral cortex (four lobes) is the center for logic.

  limbic system is the emotional brain.

  cingulate gyrus—involved in obsessive worry

  nucleus accumbens—involved in addictions

  amygdala—involved in rage and PTSD (post-traumatic stress disorder)

  hippocampus—involved in emotional memory; damaged in PTSD

  basal ganglia—caudate nucleus is involved in obsessive thoughts.

- diencephalon

thalamus—relays sensory information; the anterior nucleus functions in emotions and memory

hypothalamus—links the nervous system to the endocrine system via the pituitary gland

pituitary gland—produces hormones that help regulate other endocrine functions

- midbrain and neurotransmitter production—every psychological emotion has a physiological cause; the neurotransmitters (serotonin, dopamine, and norepinephrine) are literally linked to the chemistry of emotions; psychiatric medications work by modulating these chemicals.

- cerebellum—coordinates and regulates muscular activity; the cerebellum probably does not escape the effects of stress

dendrites

Dendrites are part of the neuron. Dendrites take messages to the neuron, and axons take messages away from the neuron. Each neuron has many dendrites. About 95 percent of the total receptive surface that neurons offer for contact to other neurons is made up of dendrites.

Experiences that can decrease dendrite arborization include age, stress, illness, and injury. Education is one of the best ways in which to increase dendritic fields.

memory

Memory processes the recall of past occurrences; involves encoding, storage, and retrieval of information; involves both short-term and long-term memory; involves both episodes (specific things that happened) and semantics (words and rules for using them); can be conscious or unconscious; and can be improved by techniques that rely on association, chunking, and rehearsal.

neurogenesis

Neurogenesis is the growth of nerve cells. It increases with:

- physical exercise, which increases oxygen to the brain
- psychological exercise or mental exercise
- psychopharmacology or drugs—antioxidants (omega-3 fatty acids); vitamins C, E, D, B_6, B_9, B_{12}; curry (curcumin) may help; lithium; anti-depressants
- less stress

neuron

A neuron is a nerve cell found in both the central nervous system and the peripheral nervous system. Neurons are composed of a cell body, nissel bodies, an axon, and dendrites. Neurotransmitters or chemical messengers are located in the synapse between neurons.

neuroplasticity

Neuroplasticity means that our brains are moldable. It is the formation of new connections between brain cells. The number of synapses between the cells (connections) can probably be increased with mental exercises and sleep.

These experiences can change brain structure and, in turn, increase memory storage.

neurotransmitters

We could not think or feel without neurotransmitters. Every psychological emotion has a physiological cause, and neurotransmitters are part of the cause.

Neurotransmitters are chemicals (made from amino acids) that transmit nerve impulses from one cell to the next. Neuropeptides (endorphins, enkephalins, dynorphins) are also neurotransmitters; they are the body's natural pain-killers.

Psychiatric medications often work by initially altering neurotransmitters, which results in changes in postreceptor sites, ion transport, secondary messenger systems, brain-derived neurotropic factor, and eventually the DNA within the nucleus of the cell.

stress and decreased memory

Stress begets more stress. Chronic stress is not easy to abate but can be decreased. People who are stressed often turn to cigarettes, drugs, and/or alcohol. These age the brain and body further. Chronic stress decreases memory and can be a risk factor for Alzheimer's disease.

Continued high cortisol from chronic stress results in decreased BDNF (brain-derived neurotrophic factor), which results in decreased neurons in the prefrontal cortex and hippocampus and thus, decreased memory.

synapses

Synapses are the junctions between nerve cells. Neurotransmitters or chemical messages are released at the presynaptic terminal of the departing axon of one nerve cell secondary to an electrical impulse. The neurotransmitter then diffuses across the gap or synapse and attaches to a postsynaptic receptor site of a receiving dendrite of another neuron.

Appendix B

Alzheimer's Disease, Dementias, and Cognition

active lifestyle and cognition

Lack of physical activity causes deterioration in brain matter volume and might be one of the most powerful lifestyle factors contributing to Alzheimer's disease. Physical activity increases brain volume; the average gray matter volume is 663 ml in those with an active lifestyle compared to 628 ml in those with an inactive lifestyle.

addictions and dementia

Addictions are common risk factors for dementia (addictions to food, inhalants, sex, nicotine/cigarettes, alcohol, prescription drugs, marijuana, methamphetamines, cocaine, party drugs, heroin, LSD, THC, etc.). For example, alcohol consumption may result in lower brain volume over time. Dependency and withdrawal result in significant physical, psychological, and social consequences.

age-associated memory impairment

Some memory decline is common in those over fifty-five years of age. Often taking the form of memory lapses, this kind of memory decline is considered normal within the limits for the age groups. Older memories and memories of personal information tend to survive well into old age. There may also be a minor decline in cognitive abilities, psychomotor skills, reaction times, performance in executive tasks, and visuospatial skills. There is little impact on daily functioning.

Alzheimer's disease—dementia

Alzheimer's dementia usually occurs after age sixty-five, but 5 percent of cases occur prior to this age. Besides age, risk factors include a positive family history, head trauma, Down syndrome, and heart disease. It is chronic with a substantial decline in at least two areas of cognitive functioning, such as aphasia (word-finding difficulties), agnosia (naming difficulties), apraxia (movement disturbances), and executive functioning.

Average survival rate is eight years after diagnosis but can span between four and twenty years. Survival may be modified significantly by interventions.

Alzheimer's dementia includes:

- brain atrophy with enlarged cerebral lateral ventricles
- abnormal procession of amyloid plaques; abnormal phosphorylation of tau protein
- destruction of Ach neurons in nucleus basalis of Meynert

- APP defect (amyloid precursor protein)—
  chromosomes 1, 14, 21; APOE defect—
  chromosome 19

Alzheimer's disease—methods of detection

- MRI (magnetic resonance imaging) may show
  volume loss from baseline, particularly in the hippocampus; shows clinical progression and predicts
  treatment outcome

- PET (positron emission tomography imaging)
    computer-assisted X-rays track a radioactive sub-
      stance inside a patient's body to study the bio-
      chemical activity of the brain
    F-fluorodeoxyglucose shows clinical progression
    PET imaging with carbon 11 detects plaques in the
      brain (best for anti-amyloid therapy consider-
      ation)

- biomarkers in cerebrospinal fluid (CSF)—tau protein and A β 42 (amino acid—β amyloid)

- genotype marker—APOE4 (E4 apolipoprotein)

- cognitive evaluation is the primary diagnostic tool
  for Alzheimer's dementia; cognitive measurements
  during clinical evaluations include evolutions of
  aphasia, apraxia, agnosia, executive function disturbance, and tremors; impaired memory retrieval;

decreased information processing, abstractions, and sequencing; and decreased organizing and planning.

Alzheimer's disease—stages of decline

- stage 1—no detectable memory problems or symptoms of dementia
- stage 2—very mild decline: aware of memory deficit; often attributed to normal aging
- stage 3—mild decline: notices memory and cognitive decline; difficulty in finding right words, remembering names, planning and organizing
- stage 4—moderate decline: difficulty with arithmetic and finances; forgets life history details; poor short-term memory
- stage 5—moderately severe decline: requires assistance with daily activities; confusion; difficulty recalling personal details
- stage 6—severe decline: needs constant supervision; apathetic, agitated, unaware; personality changes; sketchy memory of the past; loss of bladder and bowel control
- stage 7—very severe decline: final stage of the disease; noncommunicative

antihistamines and dementia

- Caution is recommended for those with dementia when using many of the antihistamines, as antihistamines can increase confusion in the elderly.

- Antihistamines have mild anticholinergic activity (anticholinergics are a class of drugs that block the action of the neurotransmitter acetylcholine in the brain), which is believed to be part of the reason why these medications increase confusion in those with dementia.
- They should also be used with caution in patients with glaucoma, benign prostatic hyperplasia, obstructive gastrointestinal tract, and bladder obstructions.

biomarkers for Alzheimer's disease (AD)

There are no definitive biomarkers, however, the following neurochemical indicators are used to assess the risk or presence of the disease:

- cerebrospinal fluid measures of beta-amyloid protein and tau protein
- MRI of brain atrophy (AD has a profound loss of neuronal cells especially in the cortex and hippocampus)
- PET visualization of beta-amyloid and glucose metabolism
- APOE4 alleles in the serum have been found.
    zero alleles—15 percent risk of AD by eighty years of age
    one allele—50 percent risk of AD by eighty years of age
    two alleles—90 percent risk of AD by eighty years of age

choice

Choice is the action of selecting by an act of the will and involves examining options and alternatives. Choices along with genetics and environment can increase or abate dementia development.

cognitive delay/impairment—tests for evaluating

With the spotlight on the baby boomers and the risk of Alzheimer's dementia, mild memory problems of early cognitive impairment—a decline in memory or thinking skills—are a concern.

Cerefolin NAC is approved for treatment of early cognitive delay. Thus, a group of vitamins and an amino acid precursor of acetylcholine have been shown to help in early memory problems.

Tools used to predict conversion to dementia include:

- clinical interview—observation of subjective memory impairment, cognitive function, and functional impairment
- blood and cerebrospinal fluid (CSF) tests—APOE4 genotype, beta-amyloid protein, CSF beta-amyloid, CSF tau protein
- neuropsychological tests—Mini-Mental Examination, Montreal Cognitive Assessment, and others
- neuroradiology tests—PET scan, MRI volumetry of hippocampus and whole brain, magnetic resonance spectroscopy (MRS)

cognitive functioning tests—examples

- *verbal memory*—fifteen words are given, and patient is asked to recall them; repeated five times.

- *working memory*—numbers of increasing size are given, and patient is asked to repeat the numbers from lowest to highest.

- *motor speed*—one hundred plastic tokens are given and patient is asked to place them into a container as quickly as possible for sixty seconds.

- *verbal fluency*—patient is given sixty seconds to name as many words as possible in a semantic category; and, in two separate trials, sixty seconds to name as many words as possible that begin with a given letter.

- *reasoning and problem solving*—patient looks at two pictures simultaneously; each picture shows three different colored balls arranged on three pegs with the balls in a specific arrangement in each picture; patient is asked to determine the fewest number of times the balls in one picture would need to be moved to make the arrangement of balls identical to that of the second picture.

- *attention and processing speed*—patient is asked to recognize simple visual patterns, take tests that require simple decision making, do basic mathematical calculations, and do reasoning tasks as quickly as possible.

- *emotional distractibility and affective memory*—patient is given twenty words: ten are nonaffective (fruits and vegetables) and ten have emotional valence (romantic or cancer); patient is given trials to recall all words, then is asked to recall the nonaffective and affective words separately.

After a delay, patient is given a recognition trial with the twenty words given earlier and twenty new words; the test allows five minutes for a recall trial and two minutes for a recognition trial.

- *emotion inhibition test*—patient is given sheets of paper with four columns of words (neutral or affective) or symbols in colored or black ink and asked to either read the words or name the colors of the ink going down the columns; thirty seconds are given for each page; the measure is the patient's ability to name colors of affective words under control conditions.

cognitive impairment due to normal aging—not dementia

- little impact on day-to-day functioning
- decline in memory or other cognitive ability; memory retrieval deficiencies
- decreased psychomotor skills, reaction time, performance on executive tasks, and visuospatial skills

dementia

Dementia is a combination of several cognitive deficits, such as impaired memory; confusion; disturbance in planning, organizing, sequencing, language, and abstracting; and impairment of ability to carry out motor activities. It can be mild initially and become severe as it progresses.

dementias—common types

Physical changes in the brain cause different forms of dementia. Coexisting conditions and overlapping symptoms and pathologies complicate diagnoses. Some dementias (a result of infections, toxins, metabolic diseases, deficiency states, normal pressure hydrocephalous in some cases) are reversible. Following are highlights of some of the most common types of dementias.

- **alcohol-induced dementia**

  typically multifactorial in those with a history of alcoholism

  Wernicke-Korsakoff syndrome results from low thiamine (B1); Wernicke encephalopathy is the first, acute phase. Difficulty walking (ataxia), abnormal eye movements (nystagmus), and cognitive dysfunction including confusion and confabulation may be seen. Korsakoff psychosis is the chronic stage.

  alcohol-induced persisting dementia is a more subtle form of dementia, it's now believed, that results from alcoholism

- **Alzheimer's disease dementia**

  Alzheimer's dementia involves diffuse atrophy of the brain cells, increased senile plaques, increased neurofibrillary tangles, increased amyloid proteins, and enlarged cerebral ventricles. Acetylcholine is the neurotransmitter of the brain most affected.

  risk factors—age (over sixty-five years), first-
    degree relative with AD, traumatic brain injury;
    early onset is more progressive

  most common dementia, 60–80 percent of demen-
    tia cases; prevalence doubles every five years
    after age sixty

  aphasia, apraxia, agnosia, decreased executive
    functioning

  senile plaques, neuronal loss, synaptic loss, granu-
    lovascular degeneration of nerves

  chromosomes 1, 14, 19, 21, APOE4

  MRI shows atrophy; genotyping sometimes done

  cerebral atrophy, ventricular enlargement

- **Creutzfeldt-Jakob disease**

  rapid, progressive, rare; caused by a transmittable
    prion

  decreased memory, personality changes, hallucina-
    tions, spasmodic jerky muscles

  spikes in EEG, symmetric, diffuse, rhythmic, slow
    waves

- **Fahr's disease dementia**

  This is a spontaneous, unknown-cause calcifica-
  tion of the basal ganglia with symptoms that can
  include Parkinsonism, abnormal involuntary movements, choroathetosis, dystonia, ataxia, dementia,
  depression, and schizophrenia-like symptoms. An
  MRI is helpful in the diagnosis.

- **frontotemporal dementias**

  A group of disorders characterized by nerve cell degeneration in the frontal lobes and temporal lobes of the brain, including Pick's disease, primary progressive aphasia, and behavioral variant frontotemporal dementia, among others. Characterized by earlier age of onset, loss of executive function and social skills, behavior changes, and problems with speech that eventually lead to mutism. Some subtypes eventually develop movement dysfunction.

  younger average age of onset

  initial symptoms—personality changes, behavior changes

  disinhibition, progressive nonfluent aphasia, semantic dementia

  corticobasal degeneration, neuronal loss, gliosis, spongiform changes, Pick's bodies present, asymmetrical focal atrophy of frontotemporal regions

  genetic linkage perhaps—chromosome 9, 17

- **human immunodeficiency virus (HIV) type 1 dementia**

  This dementia affects 10 percent of those with AIDS. AIDS is an infection of the brain by HIV. Free radicals are produced and intracellular calcium increases. Many associated organisms (toxoplasmosis, cryptococcus neoformans, cytomegalovirus, herpes simplex, varicella zoster, syphilis, TB, Kaposi's sarcoma, candida, adenovirus II, papovirus, MAC, aspergillus, coccidioides, rhizopus, acremonium, listeria, nocardia) can also cause mental changes.

AIDS dementia symptoms may include mental slowing, decreased memory and concentration, irritability, psychomotor slowing, personality changes, decreased reasoning, changes in brain chemicals and structure, muteness, eventual severe cognitive deficits, depression, mania, psychosis, and suicidal ideation.

- **Huntington's dementia**

    An autosomal dominant disease characterized by cognitive dysfunction, psychiatric symptoms, and problems with movement. Degeneration begins in the medial caudate nucleus and proceeds to the putamen. MRI will show atrophy of the caudate or putamen; PET scan will show hypometabolism in the striatum. Genetic testing is performed for final diagnosis.

    Huntington's dementia is characterized by decreased memory, decreased visuospatial abilities, decreased learning of new information, and single-word answers. Psychiatric symptoms may include personality changes, apathy, lability, impulsivity, egocentrism, decreased self-control, depression (may predate the dementia by several years), hypomania, psychosis, intermittent explosive episodes, and altered sexual behavior.

    50 percent of patients present with psychiatric symptoms (emotional or cognitive such as irritability, apathy, or depression); initial motor

symptoms may include restlessness, rigidity, jerks, ulnar deviation of the hands; later symptoms may include head bobbing, grimacing, akinesia, dystonia, psychosis, and articulation abnormalities.

chromosome 4, autosomal, dominant, trinucleotide repeat

subcortical, "boxcar" ventricles; somatostatin is increased; decreased GABA in the striatum, Ach in the striatum, and dopamine and neurokinins

choreiform (dancelike) movements, muscular hypertonicity

- **hypothyroidism-related cognitive decline**

  increased TSH, decreased T_4

  obesity, constipation, coarse hair

  lethargy, decreased mood

  slow cognitive function, memory fog

  typically reversible with treatment

- **Lewy body dementia**

  A progressive dementia caused by abnormal deposits in brain cells that cause damage over time. These deposits are called Lewy bodies and are composed of the protein alpha-synuclein. The disease is characterized by a combination of cognitive deficits as well as the following:

problems with motor features similar to Parkinson's disease: bradykinesia, cogwheel rigidity, resting tremor, shuffling gait

fluctuating cognitive impairment, visual hallucinations, delusions, misinterpretation of visual information, variation in alertness

rapid eye movement (REM) sleep disorder

dysfunction of autonomic nervous system

poor response to neuroleptics

- **neurosyphilis dementia**

  FTA-ABS (fluorescent treponemal antibody absorption blood test) checks for the presence of antibodies to Treponema pallidum bacteria, which cause syphilis; another characteristic is Argyll Robertson pupils (eyes), which refers to small pupils that reduce in size on a near object and don't constrict when exposed to bright light.

- **normal pressure hydrocephalous**

  This is a disorder that typically presents with a triad of symptoms that includes dementia/cognitive issues, gait disturbances, and urinary incontinence. Causes include obstruction of cerebrospinal fluid flow, deficiency in reabsorption of cerebrospinal fluid, subarachnoid hemorrhage, head trauma, meningitis, encephalitis, and cancer.

  cognitive issues may include decreased attention, decreased judgment, decreased new learning, and decreased visuospatial ability gait slow, short, low height (apraxia)

CT scan may show increased ventricular size and dilated cerebral ventricles; cisternography shows reflux into the ventricles

treatment includes lumbar puncture with removal of CFS or shunting

cognitive issues may be fully or partially reversible with treatment

- **Parkinson's dementia**

  often age fifty to sixty years at onset

  50 percent have depression, 35 percent have dementia

  tremor, bradykinesia, muscle rigidity

  neuronal loss in substantise niagra; subcortical

- **progressive supranuclear palsy and dementia**

  This is considered a subtype of frontotemporal dementia, but also has prominent movement symptoms. These patients show profound bradykinesia, neck rigidity, dysarthria, dysphasia, restriction of gaze, deficits in verbal memory, decreased calculating ability, slow central processing, but no agnosia, no apraxia, and no aphasia. They may exhibit apathy, emotional indifference, outbursts of rage, and OCD-like symptoms.

  There is decreased striatal dopamine and decreased acetylcholine in the cortex. Many other causes are possible (central nervous system infections, toxins, chronic subdural hematoma,

connective tissue diseases, endocrine factors, metabolic diseases, various B deficiency states, substance
abuse, hypercalcium, etc.), but the odds are great
that a dementia is either Alzheimer's or vascular dementia or a combination of both in etiology.

- **traumatic brain injury (TBI) dementia**
    A TBI is caused by a blow to the head or penetrat-
ing head injury that disrupts the functioning of the
brain; many involve motor vehicle accidents and/
or alcohol. The three most common patterns are
contusions (from falls), subdural hematomas, and
diffuse axonal injuries as from vehicle acceleration or
deceleration.

    Mild TBI may be found in postconcussion syn-
drome with brief loss of consciousness, inattention
and information-processing impairment, headaches,
fatigue, insomnia, dizziness, memory impairment,
tinnitus, sensitivity to light or sound, anxiety, depression, and irritability.

    TBI can result in dementia and is a risk factor for
        Alzheimer's disease

    TBI often considered mild if loss of consciousness
        is less than thirty minutes; however, even a brief
        loss of consciousness can decrease information
        processing

    depression, mania, schizophrenia-like symptoms,
        seizures, anxiety disorders, and aggression
        (brief, sudden, over trivial issues) may occur

TBI dementia—slowed cognitive processing; decreased attention, concentration, executive functioning, and memory; personality changes such as childishness and emotional lability; decreased interests, spontaneity, and social contact; restlessness, anxiety, and psychosis

can manifest in frontal lobe syndrome; orbitofrontal syndrome characterized by disinhibition, distractibility, and lability; dorsolateral syndrome characterized by apathy, slowness, and mutism; inferior orbital/anterior temporal syndrome characterized by rage episodes, fear, loss of inhibitions, and withdrawal

increases beta-amyloid protein, which increases risk of Alzheimer's in those with one copy of the APOE gene; norepinephrine is elevated, calcium influx causes neurotoxicity, and glutamate is increased

- **vascular dementia (multi-infarct dementia)**
  A probable diagnosis is made by noting the correlation of dementia with cardiovascular atherosclerotic disease. Multi-infarct dementia is a term for many small-vessel infarcts in different areas of the brain. The cognitive deficits are determined by the location of the infarcts. The onset of dementia may be within three months of a stroke.

  believed to be the second most common dementia

  risk factor is atherosclerotic heart disease and sequela such as hypertension

   hypertension can cause lacunar strokes or deep in-
      farctions below the cortex

   symptoms include slowness of cognition, impaired
      executive functioning, decreased memory,
      decreased visuospatial abilities, progressive lan-
      guage dysfunction, disinhibition, apathy, limited
      insight

   abrupt or stepwise onset and deterioration

   may cause gradual changes in personality and
      behavior

   focal neurological signs; characteristic depends on
      area of infarction or infarctions

   periventricular white-matter changes; MRI will
      show small subcortical infarcts; a PET scan or
      SPECT scan will show multiple small areas of
      hypometabolism

- **vitamin B_{12} deficiency dementia**
   Some forms of dementia can mirror symptoms
of a vitamin B_{12} deficiency. Unlike Alzheimer's, a B_{12}
deficiency can be reversed when treated with higher
doses of the vitamin.

- **Wilson's disease dementia**
   Wilson's disease is hepatolenticular degeneration,
an autosomal recessive (and treatable) disease. It is
a gene defect affecting chromosome 13 coding for a
protein for copper metabolism. Copper accumulates
in the basal ganglia, cornea (Kaysen-Fleischer rings
in eyes), and liver, causing symptoms by age thirty

years. Twenty-four-hour urine copper is increased and ceruloplasmin is decreased.

> hypomania, motor symptoms (tremor, rigidity, dystonia, dysarthria, dysphagia, abnormal gait), psychiatric symptoms (mild memory and executive disturbances with extrapyramidal signs, depression in 20–30 percent), decreased serum ceruloplasmin

> chromosome 13, autosomal recessive

dementia summaries—diagnosis, evaluation, differential, causes, treatments

- diagnosis

> cognitive defects—at least one of the following: aphasia (word-finding difficulties), apraxia (gait disturbance), agnosia (naming difficulties), executive functioning disturbance

> functioning impairments—social, occupational

> decline from previous level of functioning

- evaluation

> medical, neurological, psychiatric, information from caregivers

> medication evaluation for drugs that might decrease cognition including benzodiazepines, anticholinergics, beta-blockers, opioids, corticosteroids

> neuropsychological testing, laboratory data, and MRI of head

- differential

    delirium—disturbance of alertness and consciousness, disorientation, acute not chronic, fluctuation of symptoms, decreased attention to environment, increased or decreased activity and agitation, visual hallucinations; typically due to underlying medical illness

    major depressive disorder—dysphoria before cognitive impairment, anhedonia before cognitive impairment, impaired performance on neuropsychological tasks

    normal pressure hydrocephalus—cognitive issues, gait disturbance, urinary incontinence

- causes

    Alzheimer's disease—increased age, traumatic brain injury, decreased brain reserve, decreased education, cerebrovascular disease, increased lipids, increased blood pressure, increased arteriosclerotic heart disease, smoking, obesity, diabetes mellitus, atrial fibrillation, genetic predisposition

    transient ischemic attacks/vascular aspect—increased age, lipids, coronary artery disease, arrhythmias, smoking; MRI for cerebrovascular disease

    normal pressure *hydrocephalus*

    endocrine disorders—untreated hypothyroidism (decreased cognition, increased anger, increased depression, increased paranoia), hyperthyroidism, Cushing disease, Addison's disease, hypoparathyroidism, hyperparathyroidism, untreated vitamin B$_{12}$ deficiency

traumatic brain injury—head trauma can cause diffuse axonal injury with shearing forces, contusions, hemorrhages, lacerations, hypoxic ischemia; anterograde and retrograde amnesia; decreased encoding and decreased retrieval of new information, disorganized thinking, decreased concentration and fluent aphasia; dementia pugilistica (in boxers)

chronic subdural hematoma—from mild head trauma; can cause headache, slowed thinking, hemiparesis, change in personality, seizures, aphasia

infections—neurosyphilis (general paresis) with increased anger, decreased cognition, delusions, hallucinations; use fluorescent treponemal antibody test; HIV-associated dementia can be subcortical and spare cortex; increased forgetfulness, decreased concentration, slowed thinking, apathy, social withdrawal; psychosis possible; watch for central nervous system infections and concerns, and systemic illness—all can decrease cognition

toxins—alcohol long-term use; mild initially; anterograde and retrograde amnesia; decreased letter fluency, fine motor control, recall

frontotemporal dementias—onset before age sixty-five; cognitive dysfunction, speech dysfunction, behavior changes, and personality changes are characteristic

Lewy body disease—combination of cognitive dysfunction and movement dysfunction; may have coexisting Alzheimer's and vascular dementia; motor symptoms similar to those seen in Parkinson's disease; also may have visual hallucinations

Huntington's disease—trinucleotide repeat in gene on chromosome 4; autosomal dominant. Early symptoms—decreased attention, decreased concentration, decreased visuospatial ability, decreased emotional processing, decreased memory, caudate-putamen of BG involved. Late symptoms—decreased planning, decreased problem solving, decreased cognitive flexibility, increased distractibility, decreased information processing, decreased motivation, increased depression, increased apathy, increased personality changes, increased suicidal ideations, psychosis, cortical-striatal dysfunction

- treatments

  biological—drug treatment of cause

  behavioral—therapy by trained caregivers

  emotional—coping skills

  cognitive—mental stimulation exercises

  sensory stimulus—sight, smell, hearing, taste, touch

social living environment, ability to drive, safety, supervision, to-do lists, routines, cues to help memory, home safety, housekeeper, food service, financial planning, psychoeducation for caregivers, internet resources

discouragement and early cognitive delay

Discouragement is a lay term that refers to a loss of enthusiasm, confidence, and courage that may occur in early cognitive delay. Apathy, a lack of interest, enthusiasm, or concern, is more common in dementia.

early cognitive delay avoidance

The following will help to decrease the odds for early cognitive delay and preserve memory: avoid addiction or unhealthy dependencies chemically or in relationships, maintain a healthy lifestyle, decrease stress, exercise the brain, possibly delay retirement, sleep seven to eight hours per night, renew life purpose, get daily physical exercise, stay connected with people, stay thin, eat a healthy diet, increase knowledge, don't smoke or drink alcohol in excess.

laughter and cognition

- laughter can improve cognition, mood, social bonding; decrease pain and postprandial glucose level in diabetes; and improve cardiovascular functioning and immune functioning
- various brain areas are involved in laughter: left frontal superior gyrus, amygdala, hypothalamus, temporal lobe, cerebellar region, left prefrontal

cortex (more in females), mesolimbic regions (more in females)

psychiatric and dementia diagnosis in the future

Diagnosis is moving toward not being totally symptom based. Other factors will be considered, including neuroanatomy, brain imaging, molecular biology, genomic research, cognitive neuroscience, and psychopharmacology research.

Appendix C

Vocabulary Words

A friend told me how her family learned to love words: through all her years growing up, each family member was charged with using a new word sometime during daily dinner conversations. They kept a well-worn dictionary next to the kitchen for last-minute word choices. They often chose ones that would get laughs or eye rolls. It was fun to listen for the words and see how they gave mealtime conversations unexpected turns. Two generations later, her grandchildren are still enjoying this easy family game.

Easy tips for learning words:

- Learn and review words in groups of fewer than seven.
- The brain can better comprehend one-word definitions.
- Even if you already know some of the following words, practice using them more often in conversations.

- Review new words over a period of weeks to help store them in your permanent memory.

abash: to embarrass

abate: to reduce

aberrant: atypical

abet: to aid

abide: to remain

abject: sad

abridge: to shorten

abstemious: moderate in eating

abstruse: difficult to understand

absurd: ridiculous

accede: to yield

acerbic: bitter

acrid: bitter

adamant: unyielding

adept: skilled

adulation: praise

aficionado: a fan

agile: quick

al fresco: out-of-doors

altruistic: unselfish

amiable: friendly

animosity: hostility

apathy: lack of interest

aplomb: self-assurance

appease: to bring toward peace

arcane: difficult to understand

ardently: passionately

ascertain: to find out definitely

askance: with suspicion

askew: crooked

asperity: roughness of manner

aspire: desire

assail: to attack

assault: attack

assent: to agree

astute: clever

audacious: bold

augment: to increase

austere: simple

avert: to turn away

avid: eager

bailiwick: area of skill

ballyhoo: blatant advertising

banal: commonplace

bantam: small

bathos: overly sentimental

batten: to thrive

befuddle: to confuse thoroughly

beguile: to charm

benevolent: good-hearted

benign: harmless

beseech: to beg

bilk: to cheat

blandishment: flattery

blatant: showy

blithe: cheerful

bona fide: genuine

boon: a blessing
boorish: rude
brackish: having a salty taste
brandish: to flaunt
brazen: bold
brindled: streaked with a dark color
brio: liveliness
brouhaha: an uproar
bumptious: arrogant
caliber: degree of quality
callow: immature
cant: meaningless talk
capacious: roomy
capitulate: to yield
caprice: a sudden change of mind
captious: critical
careen: to cause to lean
carp: to complain
castigate: to punish
cavalier: arrogant
cavil: to find fault
chafe: to fret
chagrin: humiliation
chimera: an illusion
churl: a rude person
circa: about
circumspect: cautious
clandestine: secretive
cobble: to bind
coddle: to pamper
cognizant: aware
comestible: edible

comport: to agree
concede: to yield
concur: to agree
congregate: to gather
consternation: dismay
contentious: argumentative
contravene: to oppose
conundrum: a puzzle
convivial: sociable
copious: abundant
corpulent: fat
corroborate: to confirm
coterie: an exclusive group
covert: secretive
covet: to envy
credible: believable
credulous: believing easily
cuff: to hit
curry: to flatter
cyan: greenish blue
dalliance: flirting
dawdle: to delay
decimate: to destroy
declaim: to speak loudly
decorous: showing good taste
decorum: etiquette
deft: skilled
deleterious: harmful
delude: to deceive
dementia: a loss of mental abilities
demure: modest
denigrate: to defame, disparage
depraved: corrupt

deride: to laugh at
diffident: shy
diffuse: to scatter
diminutive: small
din: noise
dint: a blow
dire: urgent
disdain: contempt
dismiss: to send away
disparage: to belittle
dither: a state of indecision
docent: a tour guide
doleful: sad
don: to put on
dour: sad
draconian: cruel
drivel: nonsense
drone: to talk on and on
dubious: questionable
dupe: to trick
ebony: dark
eclectic: diverse
ecstatic: happy
edible: able to be eaten
effervescent: bubbling or vivacious
effuse: to pour out
egress: an exit
eke: to earn a living with difficulty
elfin: small and fairylike
elite: the best
elucidate: to make clear
elusive: evasive
emaciated: thin

eminent: famous
emulate: to imitate
enervate: to weaken
enigma: a riddle
enjoin: to forbid
enrage: to anger
entice: to attract
ephemeral: short-lived
equitable: fair
errant: wandering
eruct: to belch
et al.: and others
etc.: and so on
euphoria: a good feeling
exigent: urgent
expedite: to speed up
exposé: a disclosure
expound: to explain
expunge: to delete
extant: still existing
extinct: not existing
extol: to praise
extricate: to free
fallacious: false
fatuous: foolish
feckless: useless
feign: to pretend
feral: savage
fervent: impassioned
fetter: to hamper
flaunt: to show off
flay: to criticize
florid: colorful

flotilla: a small fleet
folderol: foolish talk
formidable: threatening
forthwith: immediately
fray: a fight
frenetic: frantic
frippery: showiness
fulminate: to explode
furtive: secretive
gaffe: a mistake
galvanize: to excite
garish: gaudy
garner: to gather
garrulous: talkative
genial: having a kind disposition
gentrify: to upgrade
germane: relevant
gerontology: study of aging
gingerly: carefully
glabrous: hairless
glaring: obvious
gloaming: dusk
gourmand: a glutton
gracious: considerate
grueling: demanding
guffaw: loud laughter
gull: to trick
gullible: easily cheated
gumption: drive
haggle: to bargain
hamper: to hinder
hapless: unfortunate
harlequin: multicolored

hebetate: to make dull
heed: to consider
helter-skelter: haphazardly
hermetic: airtight
heterogeneous: diverse
hispid: hairy
hobnob: to associate
hone: to sharpen
horde: a large crowd
hortatory: urging
hoyden: a tomboy
hyperbole: an exaggeration
idyllic: simple
i.e.: that is
ilk: a type
illusive: deceiving
imbibe: to drink
immutable: unchangeable
impart: to share
impeccable: faultless
impel: to force
impending: looming
imperial: majestic
imperious: domineering
implacable: unyielding
improvident: careless
impudent: rude
impugn: to attack verbally
inadvertent: without intention
inane: silly
incessant: unceasing
incisive: clear
inclement: stormy

incommodious: troublesome

incongruous: out of place

indeterminate: vague

indigent: poor

indignant: angry

indolent: lazy

indulgent: lenient

inept: incompetent

inevitable: unavoidable

infamous: wicked

infinite: endless

ingenious: clever

ingrate: an ungrateful person

innocuous: harmless

insatiable: never enough

inscrutable: mysterious

insidious: harmful

insipid: dull

insolent: rude

inspire: to breathe in

insufferable: intolerable

interdict: to forbid

interim: the time between periods

interlude: an intervening period of time

interrogate: to question

intractable: unmanageable

intrepid: fearless

irksome: annoying

irresolute: unable to decide

jeopardy: danger

jo: a sweetheart

jocular: joking

joust: to combat

jovial: happy

juggernaut: an irresistible force

kaput: ruined

kibitz: to give unwanted advice

kindle: to ignite

kinetic: relating to motion

klutz: an awkward person

knave: a dishonest person

kudos: praise

lacerate: to tear

laconic: using few words

lang syne: bygone days

languid: sluggish

larder: a pantry

lassitude: weariness

latent: dormant

laud: to praise

lax: loose

lenient: indulgent

lethargic: sluggish

levity: a lack of seriousness

ligature: anything that binds

limpid: clear

lissome: flexible

listless: lacking energy

loathe: to hate

locus: a place

loquacious: talkative

lull: a pause

lulu: anything remarkable

lummox: a large, awkward person

lurid: pale, gloomy

magenta: purplish red
magnanimous: generous
magnate: an influential person
magnitude: greatness
maim: to injure
maladroit: clumsy
malevolent: ill-wishing
malign: to slander
malingerer: one who fakes illness
malodorous: having a bad smell
mandate: a command
mar: to damage
maudlin: sentimental
maverick: an independent person
meager: small amount
meander: to wander casually
melee: a free-for-all
menagerie: a group of animals
mendacious: dishonest
methodical: systematic
meticulous: particular
misprize: to despise
mitigate: to relieve
mode: manner
mollify: to soothe
mollycoddle: a sissy
moniker: a nickname
mordant: sarcastic
mortify: to humiliate
multifarious: diverse
multitude: many
mundane: ordinary
muster: to gather

myriad: many
nascent: developing
natty: neatly dressed
nebbish: a nobody
nebulous: vague
nefarious: wicked
negligent: careless
negligible: insignificant
nemesis: an enemy
neophyte: a beginner
nescient: ignorant
neurosis: a nervous condition
nexus: a connection
nominal: slight
notorious: widely known unfavorably
noxious: harmful
nubile: beautiful
nudge: to pester
nugatory: ineffective
nullify: to negate
nurture: to nourish
obliterate: to destroy
obscure: little known
obsolete: out-of-date
obtrude: to eject
obtuse: stupid
obviate: to eliminate
occlude: to shut out
odyssey: a long, difficult journey
ombudsman: an advocate
ominous: threatening
onus: a burden

optimal: best
opulence: abundance
oust: to eject
overtly: openly
palaver: idle talk
palpably: obviously
palpitate: to pulsate
palter: to bicker
paltry: trivial
panacea: a cure-all
paradox: like a contradiction
parochial: limited in scope
parry: to ward off a blow
patronize: to treat as inferior
paucity: few
paw: to grope
peccadillo: a minor offense
pellucid: clear
penance: a voluntary suffering
penchant: a liking
perdition: complete loss
perdurable: everlasting
perfidious: treacherous
perfunctory: performed without care
pernicious: harmful
peruse: to study
petulant: rude
picayune: trivial
pilfer: to steal
piquant: exciting
pithy: using few words
placate: to calm

placid: calm
plenitude: plenty
plethora: many
pluvial: drizzly
pooh-bah: a self-important person
porcine: fat
portico: a porch
potable: drinkable
preclude: to prevent
preen: to dress up
presumptuous: bold
prevalent: widespread
prig: a self-righteous person
pristine: unspoiled
probity: honesty
proffer: to offer
proficient: competent
profligate: immoral
profuse: abundant
propagate: to reproduce
propinquity: nearness
propitiation: appeasement
propitious: advantageous
prosaic: dull
protract: to prolong
prowess: bravery
proxy: a substitute
puce: brownish purple
pugnacious: inclined to fight
pundit: an expert
purloin: to steal
quaff: to drink heartily
quail: to lose courage

quell: to subdue
query: a question
quintessence: typical
quip: a joke
rabble: a disorderly crowd
rail: to scold
rampike: a dead tree
rancor: anger
ransack: to search
rebuff: to criticize
recant: to recall
rectitude: honesty
recumbent: leaning back
reel: to whirl
reflexive: unthinking behavior
refute: to disprove
reiterate: to say again
remiss: negligent
remote: distant
repartee: a quick reply
replete: abundant
reprisal: retaliation
rescind: to cancel
reticence: quietness
reticent: reluctant to speak
reverie: daydream
riant: cheerful
rife: abundant
rogue: a dishonest person
roil: to agitate
roister: to revel
rookery: a breeding place for birds
rotund: plump

rout: to drive out
ruck: a large quantity
rue: to regret
ruse: a trick
ruthless: cruel
saccharine: sickeningly sweet
sagacious: wise
salubrious: healthy
salutary: healthful
sanction: to approve
sanguine: cheerful
sans: without
sated: full
scathed: harmed
schnook: a pathetic person
scintilla: a trace
screed: a monotonous speech
scrutinize: to examine closely
sear: to scorch
sedentary: staying in one place
shoal: a great quantity
shrewd: clever
shunt: to move to one side
sinister: evil
skulk: to sneak
sleek: smooth
sluggish: lazy
smite: to strike
snafu: a complete foul-up
solace: comfort in sorrow
solicit: to ask
solicitude: concern
spoof: a joke

spurious: false
squalid: dirty
squander: to spend wastefully
stalwart: strong
stentorian: loud
stigma: mark of disgrace
strident: harsh
stringent: strict
stultify: to make to appear stupid
succinct: brief
succor: to help
sullen: sad
sullied: tarnished
sumptuous: expensive
sundry: various
superfluous: unnecessary
supplant: to replace
surmise: to guess
svelte: slender
swarthy: dark-complexioned
symbiotic: together (mutually) beneficially
taboo: unacceptable
tacit: unspoken
tamp: to pack
tamper: to meddle
tangible: able to be touched or understood
taps: the evening military signal
tardy: late
tart: sharp
taut: tight
tawdry: gaudy

tawny: brownish yellow
temerity: boldness
temper: to moderate
temperate: moderate
tempestuous: stormy
tepid: lukewarm
terminate: to end
tether: a rope
throe: anguish
timorous: shy
tintinnabulation: the sound of bells ringing
titanic: large
tony: stylish
torpid: lazy
traduce: to slander
transcend: to rise above
transcribe: to record
transmit: to send
trek: to travel
trepidation: fear
truckle: to support a superior
trumpery: something showy
tryst: a meeting
tumid: swollen
tureen: a pot
turgid: swollen
tutelage: training
twerp: a silly person
tycoon: a person of great wealth
ubiquitous: everywhere
undulate: to move up and down
ungainly: clumsy

unsullied: untarnished
untrammeled: unrestrained
unwieldy: clumsy
usurp: to seize power
utilitarian: emphasizing the practical
utopia: an imaginary perfect land
utter: to express
vagary: an eccentric idea
vapid: dull
veer: to change in direction
vendetta: a bitter feud
venerable: worthy of respect
venerate: to respect
venial: forgivable
verbose: wordy
verboten: forbidden
verdant: green
vertigo: dizziness
vespers: evening prayers
vicarious: substitute
vicissitude: a change of circumstances
vigilant: watchful
vignette: a short story
vigor: force
vindicate: to clear from blame
vintage: old

virtuoso: a skilled performer
virulent: harmful
visage: the face
vista: a broad view
vivacious: lively
vivify: to quicken
vociferous: loud
voluble: talkative
voluminous: of great volume
vulnerable: open to hurt
waif: a stray
wan: pale
wane: to decrease
warrant: to justify
wary: cautious
wayfarer: a traveler
welter: turmoil
whet: to stimulate
willful: stubborn
wily: cunning
wince: to flinch
winsome: engaging
writhe: to twist
yahoo: a stupid person
yen: a strong desire
yenta: a busybody
yeoman: one who is loyal

Appendix D

Answers to Brain Boosters

Review Brain Boosters exercises often to retain the information in long-term memory.

Chapter 1—It's Your Choice

Abstract Puzzle

    Interpretation: The man looking at the portrait has no brothers or sisters. His father's son is himself. So he is the father of the man in the portrait. The man is looking at a portrait of his son.

Chapter 2—What Can Happen to Your Brain?

Historical Characters

    The characteristics are correct/true.

History of Ideas

   False. Several dates are out of order near the end.

Abstract Puzzle

   Interpretation: The one question to ask both men is,
      "What would he (the other man present) say?" The
      man who could not lie would say that the other man
      (who could not tell the truth) would point in the
      wrong direction. The man who could not tell the
      truth would say that the other man (who could not
      lie) would point in the wrong direction also—not
      that the man who could not lie would lie, but rather
      the man who could not tell the truth would lie. Thus,
      the correct direction to go would be the opposite of
      what either man or both men said.

Chapter 3—Your Aging Brain

United States Government

   The statements are correct/true.

United States Constitution

   The amendments are correct/true.

Chapter 4—Stress and Your Brain

Historical Ages

   The sequence is correct/true.

Historical Personalities

   The statements are correct/true.

Psychology and Memory Improvement
The statements are correct/true.

Chapter 5—Anxiety and Your Brain

Music
The information is correct/true.

Chapter 6—Science Offers Hope

Neurology and Psychiatry
The definitions and concepts are correct/true.
Conceptual Exercises
The correct answer for each of them is "a."

Chapter 7—Revive Your Purpose

Explorers' Passions and Purpose
The facts are correct/true.

Chapter 8—You Can Preserve Your Mind

Famous People in History
The facts are correct/true.
Math Concepts
The definitions are correct/true.
Biology Definitions
The definitions are correct/true.

Chapter 9—Homework for Life

Pictures on Coins and Bills

> Number 9 is incorrect. It was proposed to change the picture on the fifty-dollar bill to Ronald Reagan, but it didn't happen. The correct answer is Ulysses S. Grant.

Functions of the Mind

> The statements are correct/true.

English

> False. The definitions for numbers 7 and 8 (adjective and adverb) are reversed.

Chapter 10—Mental Exercise with Words

Brainteaser

1. ship/card = deck
2. tree/car = trunk
3. school/eye = pupil (exam and private are also possible)
4. pillow/court = case
5. river/money = bank (flow is possible)
6. bed/paper = sheet
7. army/water = tank
8. tennis/noise = racket
9. Egyptian/mother = mummy
10. smoker/plumber = pipe

Warm-Up Vocabulary Quiz

The correct answers are 1-C, 2-B, 3-A, 4-D, 5-A, 6-B, 7-C, 8-C, 9-C, 10-B.

Literary Classics

They are not all correct: Poe wrote "The Raven," not "The Crow."

Chapter 11—Broad Knowledge—Better Brain

General Knowledge Facts

The statements are correct/true.

Notes

Chapter 1 It's Your Choice

1. Vos Savant and Fleischer, *Brain Building*, 78.

Chapter 2 What Can Happen to Your Brain?

1. Leardi, *The Brain*.
2. Mastin, "The Human Memory."
3. USCB Science Line.
4. Cherry, "7 Myths about the Brain."
5. Mastin, "The Human Memory."
6. Helmuth, "Top Ten Myths about the Brain."
7. Sperry, "Split-brain approach to learning problems."
8. "Researchers DeBunk Myth of 'Right-brain' and 'Left-brain' Personality Traits."
9. Reuell, "Muting the Mozart Effect."
10. Cutler, Whitelaw, and Beattie, "American Perceptions of Aging in 21st Century."
11. Family Caregiver Alliance.
12. "Diseases and Conditions."
13. Lin et al., "Screening for Cognitive Impairment in Older Adults."
14. *2015 Alzheimer's Disease Facts and Figures.*
15. Ibid.
16. Ibid.
17. Ibid.
18. Vos Savant and Fleischer, *Brain Building*, 94.

Chapter 3 Your Aging Brain

1. *2015 Alzheimer's Disease Facts and Figures.*
2. "Aging Statistics."
3. Stettinius, *Inside the Dementia Epidemic.*
4. "What We Know Today about Alzheimer's Disease."
5. *2015 Alzheimer's Disease Facts and Figures.*
6. Sightings, *Sightings over 60* (blog).
7. Ibid.
8. Meynert, "Growing Old Isn't for Sissies."
9. DeMarco, "Test Your Memory for Alzheimer's and Dementia."
10. DeMarco, "The 7 Stages of Alzheimer's."
11. "Stages of Alzheimer's."
12. Wanjek, "Eye Scan May Detect Early Signs of Alzheimer's Disease."
13. Sauer, "Risk Factors for Alzheimer's."
14. Sauer, "Communication Tips for Dementia Caregivers."
15. "Caregiver's Guide to Understanding Dementia Behaviors."
16. Unless otherwise indicated, quotes listed in the Choose Well sections can be found at BrainyQuote or World Of Quotes; see the bibliography.

Chapter 4 Stress and Your Brain

1. "America's #1 Health Problem."
2. Basavaraj, Navya, and Rashmi, "Relevance of psychiatry in dermatology."
3. Razali, "Life Event, Stress and Illness."
4. Gabriel, "BDNF–Miracle-Gro for the Brain."
5. Carol Abaya coined these terms. See Abaya, "Is Your Life Being Squeezed?" Social worker Dorothy Miller created the term "sandwich generation" in 1981. Journalist Abaya categorized the different scenarios involved in being a part of the sandwich generation. She continues to study and expose what the term means as the trend grows.
6. "Energy Cost Impacts on American Families, 2001–2012."
7. Taubenberger and Morens, "1918 Influenza."
8. "Severe acute respiratory syndrome (SARS)."
9. Kane and Tomer, "Most Americans Still Driving."
10. *Wikipedia*, s.v. "History of Personal Computers."

Chapter 5 Anxiety and Your Brain

1. "Any Anxiety Disorder among Adults."
2. "Understanding the Facts."

3. Lee and Hatesohl, "Listening."

4. Swindoll, *Taking on Life with a Great Attitude.*

Chapter 6 Science Offers Hope

1. *2015 Alzheimer's Disease Facts and Figures.*

2. O'Rourke, "The Last Baby Boomers Turn 50."

3. "Forgetfulness." Also see, *2015 Alzheimer's Disease Facts and Figures.*

4. "Treatment Horizon."

5. "Advances in Research."

6. "Decade of Brain Imaging."

7. "Alzheimer's Disease Fact Sheet."

8. "Treatment Horizon."

9. Ibid.

10. Issacson, "20 Things You Need to Know about Einstein."

11. "What Is Neuroplasticity?"

12. "Discoveries in 2015."

13. "Intracellular Fluid."

14. Wong, Arcos-burgos, and Licinio, "Frontiers in Psychiatric Research."

15. Minirth and Meier, "Is Genetics a Good Excuse?," 44.

16. Minirth, *A Brilliant Mind*, 148–49.

Chapter 7 Revive Your Purpose

1. Minirth, "Reach for the Blue Skies," 39.

2. Dillinger, "#Goals to Shoot For."

3. Minirth, "Reach for the Blue Skies," 39–40.

4. "Calculators: Life Expectancy."

5. "The World."

6. Minirth and Meier, *Happiness Is a Choice*, 174.

7. Minirth, "Reach for the Blue Skies," 41.

8. Shook and Shook, *One Month to Live.*

Chapter 8 You Can Preserve Your Mind

1. Raichle and Gusnard, "Appraising the brain's energy budget."

2. Matthews, "Staying Young," 95.

3. Minirth, Meier, Flournoy, and Mack, *Sweet Dreams*, 45.

4. "Symptoms and Causes."

5. Matthews, "Staying Young," 95.

Chapter 9 Homework for Life

1. *Wikipedia*, s.v. "Traditional Education."
2. Hershbein and Kearney, "Major Decision."
3. "Employment Projections."
4. "Creating a Memory Box."
5. Congos, "9 Types of Mnemonics for Better Memory."
6. Adapted from Minirth, *A Brilliant Mind*, 129–30.

Chapter 10 Mental Exercise with Words

1. Vincent, "How many words do you need to know in a foreign language?"
2. "The Number of Words in the English Language."
3. "The Ten Best Vocabulary Learning Tips."
4. Vos Savant and Fleischer, *Brain Building*, 44.
5. Michelon, "Brain teaser to exercise your cognitive skills."
6. "Cognitive Assessment."
7. "Tests for Alzheimer's Disease and Dementia."
8. Minirth, *Boost Your Brainpower*, 27.

Chapter 11 Broad Knowledge—Better Brain

1. McKenzie, *14,000 Quips and Quotes*, 287.
2. "Knowledge Quotes."
3. LaFrance, "How Many Websites Are There?"

Chapter 12 Finish Well!

1. Reagan, "An Open Letter to Will Ferrell."
2. *Achieving the Promise*.
3. Nguyen, "Hacking into Your Happy Chemicals."
4. Swindoll, *Growing Strong in the Seasons of Life*, 47.

Appendix A The Brain and Memory

1. Portions of this material are adapted from Minirth, *Psychiatry A to Z*.

Bibliography

Abaya, Carol. "Is Your Life Being Squeezed?" The Sandwich Generation. http://www.sandwichgeneration.com/.

Achieving the Promise: Transforming Mental Health Care in America. Department of Health and Human Services. January 2003. http://store.samhsa.gov/product/Achieving -the-Promise-Transforming-Mental-Health-Care-in-America -Executive-Summary/SMA03-3831.

Administration on Aging, Administration for Community Living. http://www.aoa.acl.gov.

"Advances in Research." National Institute of Mental Health. 2016. https://www.nia.nih.gov/search/site/advances%2520 in%2520research.

"Aging Statistics." Administration for Community Living. https://aoa.acl.gov/aging_statistics/index.aspx.

"Alzheimer's Disease Fact Sheet." Alzheimer's Disease Education and Referral Center, National Institute on Aging. May 2015. https://www.nia.nih.gov/alzheimers/publication/alzheimers.

"America's #1 Health Problem." The American Institute of Stress. http://www.stress.org/americas-1-health-problem/.

"Any Anxiety Disorder among Adults." National Institute of Mental Health. 2016. www.nimh.nih.gov/health/statistics/prevalence.

Basavaraj, K. H., M. A. Navya, and R. Rashmi. "Relevance of psychiatry in dermatology: Present concepts." *Indian Journal of Psychiatry* 52, no. 3 (July–September 2010): 270–75. http://www.ncbi.nlm.nih.gov/pmc/articles/PMC2990831.

BrainyQuote, 2001–2016. http://www.brainyquote.com.

Byrd, Dr. Walter. "Road Under Construction." *Christian Psychology for Today* 6, no. 2 (Spring 1990): 5–6.

"Calculators: Life Expectancy." Social Security Administration. 2016. https://www.ssa.gov/planners/lifeexpectancy.html.

"Caregiver's Guide to Understanding Dementia Behaviors." Family Caregiver Alliance. 2016. https://www.caregiver.org/caregivers-guide-understanding-dementia-behaviors.

Cherry, Kendra. "7 Myths about the Brain." *Neuroscience and Biological Psychology*, January 8, 2016. https://www.verywell.com.

Chew, Grace. "'Tis the Season for Temptations." *Today's Better Life* (Fall/Winter 1991): 88.

"Cognitive Assessment." Alzheimer's Association. 2016. http://www.alz.org/health-care-professionals/cognitive-tests-patient.

Congos, Dennis. "9 Types of Mnemonics for Better Memory." The Learning Center Exchange. http://www.learningassistance.com/2006/january/mnemonics.html.

Cooper, Daniel H., et al., eds. *The Washington Manual of Medical Therapeutics*, 32nd ed. Philadelphia: Wolters Kluwer, 2016.

"Creating a Memory Box." Help for Alzheimer's Families. http://www.helpforalzheimersfamilies.com/alzheimers-dementia-dealing/capturing-memories/memory-box/.

Cutler, N. E., N. W. Whitelaw, and B. L. Beattie. "American Perceptions of Aging in 21st Century." National Council on the Aging. 2002.

"Decade of Brain Imaging." The Library of Congress. 2016. http://www.loc.gov/loc/brain/proclaim.html.

DeMarco, Bob. "The 7 Stages of Alzheimer's." Alzheimer's Reading Room. April 27, 2016. http://www.alzheimersread ingroom.com/2016/03/alzheimers-seven-stages-of-alzheim ers-disease.html.

———. "Test Your Memory for Alzheimer's and Dementia." Alzheimer's Reading Room. April 2016. http://www.alzheim ersreadingroom.com/2016/04/alzheimers-dementia-mem ory-test.html.

"Diagnosis of Alzheimer's Disease and Dementia." Alzheimer's Association. http://www.alz.org/alzheimers_disease_diag nosis.asp.

Dillinger, Samantha. "The Most Important Goals." Ranker. 2016. http://www.ranker.com/list/most-important-life-goals-list /samantha-dillinger.

"Discoveries in 2015." Cambridge Cognition Ltd. 2016. http:// www.cambridgecognition.com/investors/rns-announce ments/new-research-delivered-at-aaic1.

"Diseases and Conditions." Mayo Foundation for Medical Education and Research. 2016. http://www.mayoclinic.org /diseases-conditions.

Elenkov, I. J. "Neurohormonal-cytokine interactions: Implications for inflammation, common human diseases and well-being." *Neurochemistry International* 52 (2008): 40–51. http://www.uccs.edu/Documents/rmelamed/elenkov _2008_17716784.pdf.

Elenkov, I. J., and G. P. Chrousos. "Stress Hormones, T_H1/ T_H2 Patterns, Pro/Anti-inflammatory Cytokines and

Susceptibility to Disease." *Trends in Endocrinology &
Metabolism* 10, no. 9 (November 1999): 359–68. https://
www.ncbi.nlm.nih.gov/pubmed/10511695.

"Employment Projections." US Bureau of Labor Statistics, 2015.
http://www.bls.gov/EMP.

"Energy Cost Impacts on American Families, 2001–2012."
American Coalition for Clean Coal Electricity. February
2012. http://www.americaspower.org/sites/default/files
/Energy_Cost_Impacts_2012_FINAL.pdf.

Family Caregiver Alliance. 2016. https://www.caregiver.org.

"Forgetfulness." *United Healthcare Renew Magazine*, no. 5
(November 2014): 29. https://www.aarpmedicareplans.com
/corporate/aarpmedcare/pdfs/Renew_Issue5.pdf.

Foster, C., N. Mistry, P. Peddi, and S. Sharma, eds. *The
Washington Manual of Medical Therapeutics*, 33rd ed.
Philadelphia: Lippincott Williams & Wilkins, 2010.

Fowler, Richard. "Facing Our Fears." *Today's Better Life* (Spring
1992): 74, 77.

Gabriel, Linda. "BDNF—Miracle-Gro for the Brain." Thought
Medicine. May 2010. http://thoughtmedicine.com/2010
/05/bdnf-miracle-gro-for-the-brain.

Goldberg, Stephen. *Clinical Physiology Made Ridiculously Simple*.
Miami: MedMaster, Inc., 2004.

Gómez-Isla, T., J. L. Price, D. W. McKeel Jr., J. C. Morris, J. H.
Growdon, and B. T. Hyman. "Profound loss of layer II
entorhinal cortex neurons occurs in very mild Alzheimer's
disease." *Journal of Neuroscience* 16, no. 14 (July 15, 1996):
4491–500. https://www.ncbi.nlm.nih.gov/pubmed/8699259.

Goroll, Allan, and Albert G. Mulley. *Primary Care Medicine:
Office Evaluation and Management*, 5th ed. Philadelphia:
Lippincott Williams & Wilkins, 2006.

Helmuth, Laura. "Top Ten Myths about the Brain." *Science-Nature.* May 19, 2011. http://www.smithsonianmag.com/science-nature/top-ten-myths-about-the-brain-178357288/.

Hershbein, Brad, and Melissa S. Kearney. "Major Decision: What Graduates Earn Over Their Lifetimes." The Hamilton Project. September 29, 2014. http://www.hamiltonproject.org/papers/major_decisions_what_graduates_earn_over_their_lifetimes/.

Hirsch, E. D., Jr., Joseph F. Kett, and James Trefil. *The Dictionary of Cultural Literacy.* Boston: Houghton Mifflin, 1988.

Hollander, Eric, Martin Evers, and Cheryl M. Wong. *Contemporary Diagnosis and Management of Common Psychiatric Disorders.* Longboat Key, FL: Handbooks in Health Care, 2000. http://www.hhcbooks.com/psychiatric_disorders/contemporary_diagnosis_and_management_of_common_psychiatric_disorders.

"Intracellular Fluid: Definition & Composition." Study.com. 2016. http://study.com/search/text/academy.html?q=Intracellular+fluid%3A+definition+%26+composition+chapter+12+lesson+8#/topresults/Intracellular%20fluid:%20definition%20&%20composition%20chapter%2012%20lesson%208.

Issacson, Walter. "20 Things You Need to Know about Einstein: Childhood." *Time* (April 5, 2007). http://content.time.com/time/specials/packages/article/0,28804,1936731_1936743_1936745,00.html?iid=sr-link1.

Josephson, S. Andrew, and S. Claiborne Johnston. "Neurology Editors' Choice: Top Stories of 2013." *Journal Watch* 15, no. 5 (December 31, 2013). http://www.jwatch.org/na32964/2013/12/31/neurology-editors-choice-top-stories-2013.

Kane, Joseph, and Andie Tomer. "Most Americans Still Driving, but New Census Data Reveal Shifts at the Metro Level."

Brookings. September 29, 2014. https://www.brookings.edu
/blog/the-avenue/2014/09/29/most-americans-still-driving
-but-new-census-data-reveal-shifts-at-the-metro-level/.

Kaplan, Harold, and Benjamin A. Sadock. *Kaplan & Sadock's Pocket Handbook of Clinical Psychiatry*, 5th ed. Philadelphia: Lippincott Williams & Wilkins, 2010.

"Knowledge Quotes." BrainyQuote, 2016. https://www.brainy
quote.com/quotes/topics/topic_knowledge.html.

LaFrance, Adrienne. "How Many Web-sites Are There?" *The Atlantic*, September 30, 2015. http://www.theatlantic.com
/technology/archive/2015/09/how-many-websites-are
-there/408151/.

Leardi, Janette. *The Brain*. New Rochelle, NY: Benchmark Education Company, January 1, 2011. https://books.google
.com/books?id=Y68mvYtNjYEC&printsec=frontcover#v
=onepage&q&f=false.

Lee, Dick, and Delmar Hatesohl. "Listening: Our Most Used Communication Skill." The University of Missouri, 2015. http://extension.missouri.edu/p/CM150.

Lieberman, Jeffrey, and Allan Tasman. *Handbook of Psychiatric Drugs.* Chichester, West Sussex, England: John Wiley & Sons, 2006.

Lin, J. S., E. O'Connor, R. C. Rossom, L. A. Perdue, B. U. Burda, M. Thompson, and E. Eckstrom. "Screening for Cognitive Impairment in Older Adults: An Evidence Update for the U.S. Preventive Services Task Force." Agency for Healthcare Research and Quality. November 2013. https://www.ncbi
.nlm.nih.gov/books/NBK174643/.

Marieb, Elaine N., and Katja Hoehn. *Human Anatomy and Physiology*, 8th ed. San Francisco: Benjamin Cummings, 2010.

Mastin, Luke. "The Human Memory." 2010. http://www.human
-memory.net/brain_neurons.html.

Matthews, Dale. "Staying Young." *Today's Better Life* (Summer 1992): 93–95.

McKenzie, E. C. *14,000 Quips and Quotes for Writers and Speakers*. Grand Rapids: Baker Books, 1980.

McPhee, Stephen J., Maxine A. Papadakis, and Michael W. Rabow, eds. *Lange 2011: Current Medical Diagnosis & Treatment*, 50th ed. New York: McGraw Hill Medical, 2010.

Merriam-Webster's Medical Dictionary, new edition. Springfield, MA: Merriam-Webster, Inc., 2006.

Meynert, Barbara. "Growing old isn't for sissies." Sage Vita. January 10, 2013. http://www.sagevita.com/learning/grow ing-old-isnt-for-sissies/.

Michelon, Pascale. "Brain teaser to exercise your cognitive skills: Where do words go?" SharpBrains. June 20, 2014. http://sharp brains.com/blog/2014/06/20/brain-teaser-to-exercise-your -cognitive-skills-where-do-words-go/.

Minirth, Frank. *Boost Your Brainpower*. Grand Rapids: Revell, 2010.

———. *A Brilliant Mind: Proven Ways to Increase Your Brainpower*. Grand Rapids: Revell, 2007.

———. *In Pursuit of Happiness: Choices That Can Change Your Life*. Grand Rapids: Revell, 2004.

———. "Our Treasure Chest of Memories." *Today's Better Life* (Winter 1992): 74–77.

———. *Psychiatry A to Z, 2013 Edition of Psychopharmacology Words and Concepts Every Student of Psychopharmacology Should Know*. Unpublished manuscript, 2010.

———. "Reach for the Blue Skies." *Today's Better Life* (Spring 1993): 39–41.

———. "Relax." *Today's Better Life* (Premiere Issue, 1991): 54–58.

———. "When Opportunity Whispers." *Today's Better Life* (Fall 1993): 70–72.

Minirth, Frank, and Paul Meier. *Happiness Is a Choice.* Grand Rapids: Baker Books, 1988.

———. "Is Genetics a Good Excuse?" In *Happiness Is a Choice.* Grand Rapids: Baker Books, 1988.

Minirth, Frank, Paul Meier, Richard Flournoy, and Jane Mack. *Sweet Dreams.* Grand Rapids: Baker Books, 1985.

Minirth, Frank, John Reed, and Paul Meier. *Beating the Clock.* Richardson, TX: Today Publishers, 1985.

Morley, Patrick M. "God's Blueprint for Living." *Today's Better Life* (Fall 1992): 91–92.

Naser, Suhayl. "No laughing matter: Laughter is good psychiatric medicine." *Current Psychiatry* 12, no. 8 (August 2013): 20. http://www.mdedge.com/currentpsychiatry/article/76797 /bipolar-disorder/no-laughing-matter-laughter-good-psych iatric.

Nasrallah, Henry A., ed. *Current Psychiatry* 12, no. 4 (March 2013).

National Center for Biotechnology Information. US National Library of Medicine. http://www.ncbi.nlm.nih.gov/books.

National Council on the Aging. https://www.ncoa.org.

National Institute of Mental Health. http://www.nimh.nih.gov /index.shtml.

National Institute on Aging. https://www.nia.nih.gov.

National Institutes of Health. https://www.nih.gov.

Neal, Connie. "Seven Secrets for Surviving Stress." *Today's Better Life* (Winter 1993): 77–80.

Neaves, Noe. "The Endangered Elderly." *Christian Psychology for Today* 6, no. 2 (Winter 1991): 27–28.

Nguyen, Thai. "Hacking into Your Happy Chemicals: Dopamine, Serotonin, Endorphins, & Oxytocin." The Utopian Life. October 10, 2014. http://theutopianlife.com/2014/10/14 /hacking-into-your-happy-chemicals-dopamine-serotonin -endorphins-oxytocin/.

"Normal Aging vs Dementia." Alzheimer Society Canada. August 27, 2015. http://www.alzheimer.ca/en/About -dementia/What-is-dementia/Normal-aging-vs-dementia.

"100 Fascinating Facts You Never Knew about the Human Brain." Nursing Assistant Central. December 31, 2008. http://www.nursingassistantcentral.com/blog/2008/100 -fascinating-facts-you-never-knew-about-the-human-brain/.

O'Rourke, P. J. "The Last Baby Boomers Turn 50." *AARP, The Magazine* (December 2014–January 2015). http://www.aarp .org/politics-society/history/info-2014/youngest-baby -boomers-turn-50.html.

Raichle, Marcus E., and Debra A. Gusnard. "Appraising the brain's energy budget." Proceedings of the National Academy of Sciences 99, no. 16 (2002): 10237–39. http://www.pnas .org/content/99/16/10237.full.

Razali, Salleh Mohd. "Life Event, Stress and Illness." *Malaysian Journal of Medical Sciences* 15, no. 4 (October 2008): 9–18. https://www.ncbi.nlm.nih.gov/pmc/articles/PMC3341916/.

Reagan, Patti Davis. "An Open Letter to Will Ferrell." Books by Patti Davis. April 28, 2016. http://booksbypattidavis.com /an-open-letter-to-will-ferrell.

Reese, Randy. "Growing Old Gracefully." *Today's Better Life* (Spring 1992).

"Researchers DeBunk Myth of 'Right-brain' and 'Left-brain' Personality Traits." University of Utah Health Care. August 14,

2013. http://healthcare.utah.edu/publicaffairs/news /2013/08/08-14-2013_brain_personality_traits.php.

Reuell, Peter. "Muting the Mozart effect." *Harvard Gazette*, December 11, 2013. www.news.harvard.edu/gazette/story /2013/12/muting-the-mozart-effect/.

Sadock, Benjamin J., Virginia A. Sadock, and Pedro Ruiz. *Kaplan & Sadock's Study Guide and Self-Examination Review in Psychiatry*, 9th ed. Philadelphia: Lippincott Williams & Wilkins, 2011.

Sauer, Alissa. "Communication Tips for Dementia Caregivers." *Alzheimers.net* (blog), September 8, 2014. http://www.alzhei mers.net/9-8-14-dementia-communication-tips/.

———. "Risk Factors for Alzheimer's." *Alzheimers.net* (blog). December 23, 2013. http://www.alzheimers.net/2013-12-23 /risk-factors-for-alzheimers/.

Segerstrom, S. C., and G. E. Miller. "Psychological stress and the human immune system: a meta-analytic study of 30 years of inquiry." *Psychology Bulletin* 130, no. 4 (July 2004): 601–30. https://www.ncbi.nlm.nih.gov/pubmed/15250815.

"Severe acute respiratory syndrome (SARS)." MedlinePlus. Updated February 2, 2015. https://medlineplus.gov/ency /article/007192.htm.

Shook, Kerry, and Chris Shook. *One Month to Live*. Colorado Springs: WaterBrook Press, 2008.

Sightings, Tom. *Sightings over Sixty* (blog). January 6, 2015. http://sightingsat60.blogspot.com/.

Sperry, Roger W. "Split-brain approach to learning problems." In Quarton, Melnechuk, and Schmitt, *The Neurosciences: A Study Program*. New York: Rockefeller University Press, 1967, 714–22. people.uncw.edu/puente/sperry/sperry papers/#1967.

"Stages of Alzheimer's." Alzheimer's & Dementia, Alzheimer's Association. 2016. http://www.alz.org/alzheimers_disease_stages_of_alzheimers.asp.

Stahl, Stephen M. *Stahl's Essential Psychopharmacology, Neuroscientific Basis and Practical Application*, 4th ed. New York: Cambridge University Press, 2013.

Starkstein, Sergio E., and Romina Mizrahi. "The Diagnosis of Depression in Alzheimer's Disease." *Directions in Psychiatry* 27, no. 1 (2007): 43–50.

Stettinius, Martha. *Inside the Dementia Epidemic: A Daughter's Memoir*. Horseheads, NY: Dundee-Lakemont Press, 2012. http://www.insidedementia.com/about-dementia.

Swindoll, Charles R. *Taking on Life with a Great Attitude*. Communicating Biblical Truths. Wheaton: Tyndale, n.d.

———. *Growing Strong in the Seasons of Life*. Portland, OR: Multnomah, 1983.

"Symptoms and Causes." Mayo Foundation for Medical Education and Research. 2016. http://www.mayoclinic.org/diseases-conditions/alzheimers-disease/symptoms-causes/dxc-20167103.

Taubenberger, J., and David M. Morens. "1918 Influenza: The Mother of All Pandemics." *Emerging Infectious Diseases Journal* 12, no. 1 (January 2006). https://wwwnc.cdc.gov/eid/article/12/1/05-0979_article.

"The Number of Words in the English Language." The Global Language Monitor. November 24, 2016. http://www.languagemonitor.com/global-english/no-of-words/.

"The Ten Best Vocabulary Learning Tips." Sheppard Software. 2016. http://www.sheppardsoftware.com/vocabulary_tips.htm.

"The World: Life Expectancy (2017)." geoba.se. http://www
.geoba.se/population.php?pc=world&type=15.

Toor, Ramanpreet, Benjamin Liptzin, and Steven Fischel.
"Hospitalized, elderly, and delirious: What should you do for
these patients?" *Current Psychiatry* 12, no. 8 (August 2013):
10–18. http://www.mdedge.com/currentpsychiatry/article
/76790/alzheimers-cognition/hospitalized-elderly-and-deli
rious-what-should.

Tortora, Gerard J., and Bryan H. Derrickson. *Principles of
Anatomy and Physiology*, 12th ed. Hoboken, NJ: John
Wiley & Sons, 2009.

"Treatment Horizon: The hope for future drugs." Alz.org Research
Center. http://www.alz.org/research/science/alzheimers
_treatment_horizon.asp.

2015 Alzheimer's Disease Facts and Figures 11, no. 3. Alzheimer's
Association. https://www.alz.org/facts/downloads/facts
_figures_2015.pdf.

UCSB Science Line. http://www.scienceline.ucsb.edu.

"Understanding the Facts of Anxiety Disorders and Depression
Is the First Step." Anxiety and Depression Association of
America. Updated May 2014. https://www.adaa.org/under
standing-anxiety.

U.S. Department of Health and Human Services. https://www
.usa.gov/federal-agencies/u-s-department-of-health-and
-human-services.

Vincent. "How many words do you need to know in a foreign
language?" *Street-Smart Language Learning* (blog). February
11, 2013. http://www.streetsmartlanguagelearning.com
/2013/02/how-many-words-does-average-native.html.

Vos Savant, Marilyn, and Leonore Fleischer. *Brain Building in Just
12 Weeks.* New York: Bantam Books, 1990. http://marilynvos
savant.com.

Wanjek, Christopher. "Eye Scan May Detect Early Signs of Alzheimer's Disease." LiveScience. May 5, 2016. http://www .livescience.com/54659-eye-scan-may-detect-early-alzhei mers.html.

"What Is Neuroplasticity? Definition & Concept." Study.com. http://study.com/academy/lesson/what-is-neuroplasticity -definition-depression-quiz.html.

"What We Know Today about Alzheimer's Disease." Alz.org Research Center. http://www.alz.org/research/science/alz heimers_disease_treatments.asp.

Wikipedia. s.v. "History of Personal Computers." Last modified January 8, 2017. https://en.wikipedia.org/wiki/History _of_personal_computers.

———. s.v. "Traditional Education." Last modified December 14, 2016. https://en.wikipedia.org/wiki/Traditional_ education.

Wong, Ma-li, Mauricio Arcos-burgos, and Julio Licinio. "Frontiers in Psychiatric Research." *Psychiatric Times*, June 1, 2008. http://www.psychiatrictimes.com/login?referrer=http %3A//www.psychiatrictimes.com%2Ffrontiers-psychiatric -research.

World Of Quotes: Quotes, Sayings, and Proverbs. 2013. www .worldofquotes.com.

Yager, Joel. "Predicting Medication Response in Older Depressed Patients." *Journal Watch* 19, no. 6 (June 2013). http://www.jwatch.org/jp201304290000001/2013/04/29 /predicting-medication-response-older-depressed.

Dr. Frank Minirth passed away in 2015. He was an internationally known psychiatrist, author, and radio personality, and his successful medical practice was distinguished by the integration of Christian principles into mental health care. He was president of the Minirth Clinic in Richardson, Texas.

For over forty years Dr. Minirth helped people find a healthy balance in their lives—spiritually, psychologically, physiologically, and emotionally—through the Minirth Clinic. The clinic's motto, "A Matter of Caring," embodied his approach to treatment. He was a kind, intelligent medical doctor, theologian, family man, author, media personality, professor, and poet.

A native of Arkansas, Dr. Minirth received his Medical Doctorate and psychiatry residency certification from the University of Arkansas. He later earned a Doctorate in Theology. For years he served as an adjunct professor at Dallas Theological Seminary. An ordained minister, he was dedicated to Scripture memorization throughout his life.

He was board certified as a Diplomate of the American Board of Psychiatry and Neurology and the American Board of Forensic Medicine. He was also one of only 122 North American physicians certified by the American Society of Clinical Psychopharmacology.

Affiliations throughout his career included American Mensa, the Navigators, the American Association of Christian

Counselors, Dallas Theological Seminary, and others, and he served as a consultant to numerous hospital mental health care programs nationwide.

Dr. Minirth was the author or coauthor of over seventy books, including the bestseller *Happiness Is a Choice*, and his self-help books addressed common psychology, counseling, mental health, and family relationship issues from a biblical perspective. He wrote fifty self-help workbooks and three medical reference dictionaries on psychiatry, pain relief, and dementia. Over five million of his books are in print, with some translated into other languages.

A pioneer in Christian-based mental health care, he treated patients from all over the world who sought his distinctive care. At the time of his death, he was licensed to practice medicine in fourteen states. Dr. Minirth cohosted weekday radio and television programs for many years. The nationwide, live call-in radio programs were especially popular because of the practical applications to individuals' lives.

He was married to Mary Alice for over forty years and enjoyed time with his five grown daughters and their families at their vacation ranch in the Arkansas mountains.

As a child, I attended an idyllic, beautiful little white church in a grove in the country. Sunday after Sunday, I heard legions of sermons on various topics, including the love of Christ, grace, growing in faith, and the benefits of avoiding sin. But I didn't learn a lot about heaven.

What about heaven? It's the most beautiful, amazing place our minds can imagine. The Bible tells us what heaven is like, gives detailed descriptions, and promises it as an eternal home for all believers.

We will meet again in heaven.

Frank Minirth

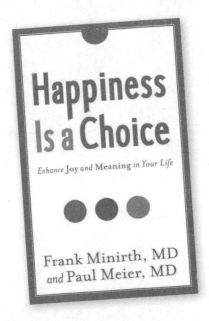